ROVERS OF THE NIGHT SKY

ROVERS OF THE NIGHT SKY

BY
"NIGHT-HAWK," M.C.

AUTHOR'S FOREWORD

THIS record of adventures—some grim, some gay—is made without pretence. To those with whom I served in France I trust it will bring back memories of our work together; of the red glow of that big factory which guided us home from many a distant raid; of "Slag-heap Sam" whose glory will never fade so long as there remains a man alive who saw him spitting his tracer-bullets into the night sky; of the hangars we fired and the dumps we missed; of "Lighthouse Luke" and "Reckless Reggie" and "The Flappers' Ruin," and all the host of them; of our raids into Hunland, and our "rags" in the mess; in fact, of all that went to make up the life of one of the best and luckiest squadrons in France.

To my general readers I can only say that this is a blunt narrative. To fly is more fascinating than to read about flying. Doubtless the whole world will fly before many years have passed. But for the moment most people have to be content to read about it. I trust, therefore, that these sketches of the War in the Air during a very critical period of our fortunes in France will serve to convey fairly just impressions of what has been done by our night-bombers.

Many of these sketches have already appeared in article form in the *Daily Mail*, *The War Illustrated*, and *Flying*, and I gladly acknowledge the courtesy of the editors of these journals in granting me permission to incorporate them in my book.

"NIGHT-HAWK."

London, Nov., 1918.

CONTENTS

CHAPTER	PAGE
1. Three " Gravel-crunchers "	1
2. Training	7
3. A " Zeppelin " Patrol	12
4. " Crashed "	17
5. First " Flips " in France	25
6. My First Bombing Raid	30
7. Testing the Weather	35
8. The Luck of " Lighthouse Luke "	41
9. On Wings of Happy Chance	46
10. Our Comic Crash	54
11. We get a New Machine	62
12. Our First Gun Raid	68
13. We " strafe " a Train	76
14. Sentinel Searchlights	80
15. My Longest Flight	86
16. The Technical Staff	93
17. Hints	102
18. " Bobby " is Missing	110
19. Little Comedies	121
20. Before the Offensive	131

Contents

CHAPTER		PAGE
21. A Strenuous Night	. . . .	134
22. Two Tragedies	. . . .	148
23. Aerial Combats in the Moonlight	. .	151
24. The Huns bomb Us	. . . .	160
25. The Story of the Prisoners' Cage	. .	165
26. How England goes to War	. . .	169
27. A Race with Dawn	. . . .	179
28. For what did He Die?	. . .	186
29. "A Miss is as Good as a Mile"	. .	192
30. Adieu!	. . . . . .	200

ROVERS OF THE NIGHT SKY

CHAPTER I

THREE "GRAVEL-CRUNCHERS"

IN a field about half-way between Arras and Vimy we made up our minds to join the Flying Corps. There were three of us—McDaniell, Boyd, and myself. We were lying in the strong sunshine outside our canvas bivouac. The battalion had just been relieved. It had been taken out of the line on the preceding evening, had trudged back to rest-billets in front of Arras, and was now expecting a move still farther back.

The afternoon was quiet. Both sides seemed to have decided that it was too hot to have a war, and save for the whine and crump of an occasional "heavy" one would not have known that there were any Huns within a thousand miles.

Mac was writing home; Boyd smoked an old pipe lazily, with long puffs and longer thoughts between them. I remember that, in watching the two of them, I dozed.

Rovers of the Night Sky

Suddenly—with that unexpectedness to which one gets accustomed in war—I woke to the realisation of a vast change. An empty, brazen sky had rapidly become filled with aeroplanes, silver in the sunshine, darting here and there in an aerial maze, the intricacies of which one could not follow. The whole earth seemed full of resonance—the song of the engines as they hummed and droned above us, the "woufs" of anti-aircraft guns, the sharp spitting of machine-guns in the sky.

We were standing up now, watching intently a great aerial battle. So far as we could see from the ground there were half a dozen of our machines and at least fifteen Huns. Our machines were two-seater fighters; the Germans were mostly single-seater scouts. For two or three minutes neither side seemed to gain any advantage; and so rapid were the turns and dives and "zooms" of the machines that only occasionally could one glimpse their distinctive markings—the black crosses of the enemy, the tricoloured circles of our own machines.

Then this drama of the sky fulfilled itself in swift tragedy. Two German and one of our own machines came down in flames, pitiably out of

Three "Gravel-Crunchers"

control, " stalling " and fluttering like leaves from autumn trees, finally—when fuselage and wings had burned themselves out—dropping like stones. A few seconds later another of our two-seaters came down, crashing into a brickfield two or three hundred yards in the rear of our position. Amazedly, and with relief, we watched the figures of both pilot and observer rise out of the ruins of their machine and walk across the field towards us.

The sky emptied as suddenly as it had filled. We watched the Germans making for their lines. A mile to our right a solitary artillery-observation machine of ours was pluckily " sitting " on some Hun " archie " doing a " shoot " for our gunners.

Then once again the sky became a blank, brazen void.

" Cheerio ! " said Mac. " The war has stopped. Let's have tea." And it was he who first touched on the subject of our transferring to the Flying Corps.

" I've had eighteen months' 'gravel-crunching,' I want to fly," he said ; then a moment after —" By Jove, I remember the Base-Adjutant reading out a notice about the shortage of observers and asking for volunteers from officers who had seen service in the line. Let's go, you fellows, and see the C.O. about it."

We went, and the upshot of it was that a week or two later a merry trio journeyed by train to Hazebrouck, that old Flanders town, which was then quite a gay old place, but has now been badly punished by shell fire and bombing. At Hazebrouck we were interviewed by a travelling commissioner of the R.F.C. who wanted to know how many times we had been " over the top," what games we played, whether we could ride, or sail a yacht, and what our motives were in seeking a transfer from the infantry. In the end he told us that we should be " applied for," that the application would take ten days or a fortnight to " go through," by which time we might expect to start on our way home to England for training.

We left the commissioner's little office feeling that we were no longer "gravel-crunchers." At dinner that evening we toasted the R.F.C.

" We'll be walking down Grafton Street, Dublin, in three weeks' time, boys," said Freddy Boyd, already visioning ahead. We were in an Irish regiment, and Dublin was our rendezvous. Boyd settled down to his pipe, and I think I know

Three "Gravel-Crunchers"

of what he was dreaming. Mac and I went out into the quiet, cobbled, moonlit streets of the old Flemish town and walked up and down, smoking, talking, listening to the dull rumbling of a barrage up "Wipers" way.

Dear old Freddy! You cannot lift your glass with mine to-night, old man! And the inimitable Mac! You, too, have ridden your horse down the long Valley of Shadows, leaving behind you only the echoes of your laughter and gaiety, and the remembrance of those good days of our unfailing comradeship.

A week after Hazebrouck we went back into the line. Curiously enough, Freddy and I were chosen by the C.O. to go up a day in advance in order to "take over the battalion frontage." We marched up on a hot afternoon, through Arras to the trenches in front of Oppy Wood. I said goodbye to Boyd in the railway cutting near the ruins of Bailleul station; and I remember him swinging away with his men across the plain towards Oppy Wood. Dusk had just fallen, and there was a slight ground-mist over the plain.

"Grafton Street on Sunday week, old bean!" Freddy shouted cheerfully.

Half an hour later he was dead—all his wonderful life and vitality quenched by a senseless bullet. A sniper got him as he was inspecting his new posts. Mercifully it was a clean shot through the brain; it brought neither pain nor regrets.

Mac and I got our papers within four days of Freddy's death. We came home to England together, and did our training together at the same school of aerial gunnery. Then Mac was sent back to France as an observer on Bristol Fighters. I was detailed for a further period of training as a night-flying observer. I had one letter from Mac describing his first impressions with his squadron in France. Within a week he had " downed " a couple of Huns.

Then came the terrible news that he, too, was dead after one of the most gallant aerial fights of the war. He and his pilot had been attacked by nearly a dozen fast enemy scouts. They managed to shoot two of them down before they themselves were sent down in flames.

The Germans buried them with honour. I have seen a photograph of their grave. The inscription on it is: " To Two Brave Men."

CHAPTER II

TRAINING

MAC and I, as I have said, came home together, and, after a few days' leave, were posted to a school of military aeronautics. The work at the school was theoretical, consisting of lectures on the general duties of observers, the different types of machines and the uses to which each type is put, map-reading, the compass, instruments, equipment, Morse signalling, and wireless. At the end of a fortnight we were sent down to an aerial gunnery school on the south coast.

For the first ten days of this course we spent most of our time on the ranges, firing, taking to pieces, cleaning, reassembling our Lewis guns. I have my card of tests now, and it evokes many a pleasant memory of those strenuous days on the ranges by the sea. I see that there were over forty tests to pass before we could leave the ground section. Mac managed to get through a couple of days ahead of me and went for his joy-ride on the day that I negotiated my final test. In mess that night his vivid impressions fired me, and I longed eagerly for my first flight.

The day came at last. Some twenty of us were motored out to the training aerodrome three or four miles along the coast. The people of the villages and hamlets we passed through were not yet astir. Not a light burned in their houses. The stars hung over the sand-dunes in a moonless sky, across which slowly drifting wracks of light, fantastic clouds passed from east to west, heaving away from the dawn. Later, in the growing light, we saw two or three sleepy rustics passing out into the fields to work.

There was a vigorous, healthy nip in the atmosphere, and we were glad to turn up the collars of our flying coats. At the aerodrome we were given numbers, instructed to report to the officer in charge of flying, and to receive from him details concerning the machines we were to fly and the "practices" we were to carry out.

"One of our machines had a forced landing yesterday afternoon," said the officer in charge of flying to me. "It is lying somewhere over there"—pointing vaguely in the direction of America.

Training

"It is several miles away. You will go out in a car with Sergeant A. The mechanics have tinkered the machine up, and Sergeant A will *endeavour* to fly it back. Oh, you needn't be windy. You've got one of the best pilots in England."

I grinned fatuously and walked away to find my pilot.

On the way out to the "initiation ceremony" Sergeant A seemed pessimistic as to our prospects of coming home again. "Engine gone to pot," he asserted. "Doubt if the wretched thing will fly at all—or, if she does, she'll probably peter out after a mile or two, and we'll have to find another field to perch in."

I thanked him for cheering me up, and we proceeded gloomily to the scene of action. He ran the engine up. To my uninitiated intelligence she appeared to be "going strong." I turned round suddenly in my seat, and caught him jerking his head in my direction and grinning at the mechanics. It may have been imagination, but I fancied the lips of one of the latter framed the words, "New observer! First flight!" Then I saw through the game and entered into the fun of it, determined that no amount of switchbacking should cause me to part company with the very excellent breakfast I had had an hour earlier. The chocks were jerked away, and the machine commenced to taxi slowly along the ground. My next impression was that we were approaching the high brick wall of a farmhouse with alarming rapidity. For two or three horrible moments I saw myself flattened out between the machine and that wall. Then suddenly my eyes evinced a tendency to fall out, the interior portion of my anatomy seemed to gravitate towards my boots, and my head appeared to be supporting a weight of at least a ton.

A second or two later we were two hundred feet above the farmyard and, as we turned, I caught a glimpse of the group of mechanics staring up at us from the field we had just left. The pilot had held the nose of the machine down as long as he safely could, gaining speed the whole time, and had then " zoomed " out of the field.

We arrived over the aerodrome at a height of about four thousand feet. " Going to spin," the pilot shouted. " Sit tight! " The sensation of spinning from the front seat of a pusher machine is one of immense pressure on the head. Meanwhile you glue your eyes on to one fixed spot on

Training

the ground beneath you, while every other feature on the landscape appears to revolve round this spot. You notice, with a kind of detached interest, that the ground is getting nearer; the earth, in fact, seems to be *coming up* to meet you. My first flight ended in a perfectly tame manner. We made a good landing and taxied up to the sheds. A blasé sergeant met us there. "Are you Mr. X?" he asked. On hearing that his surmise was correct, he handed me what looked like a machine-gun, and said : "You are to do No. 1 camera-gun test, sir. That's the machine over there—just being run up."

What to me had been a new and amazing experience appeared to that sergeant-instructor merely an ordinary routine incident of his daily life, a thing not worth commenting on.

CHAPTER III

A "ZEPPELIN" PATROL

OUR flying course on the south coast lasted about three weeks. We began with camera-gun practices designed to teach us the theory of "deflection"—that is, the amount one has to "aim off" owing to the fact that one is firing from a rapidly-moving body at another body travelling with considerable velocity either towards or away from one. We took our camera-guns up and fired them at every machine we came near. Instead, however, of sending forth a stream of bullets our guns *photographed* the machines we aimed at; and later, when the films were developed, we were able to see if we had hit any vulnerable parts. We were thus able to analyse our practices and to correct faults of "deflection."

Following this we passed on to aerial combats, reconnaissance and machine-gunning of ground targets. In those days an old R.E. 7 machine would fly up and down a defined stretch of the

A "Zeppelin" Patrol

coast—about a quarter of a mile out to sea—towing behind it a large toy-balloon. We went up in turns on a Vickers Fighter, and from the front seat endeavoured to "get" the balloon with tracer-ammunition from our Lewis guns. I confess to a great admiration for the pilot of that R.E. 7. It is no joke being "potted at" for two hours at a stretch by embryo observers. On two occasions while I was there the R.E. 7 landed in haste on the aerodrome, and the pilot, jumping out, sarcastically inquired if the last "blinking blank" who had fired at him had mistaken him for a marauding Gotha or a Fokker scout. Fortunately there were no casualties. It was alleged that shots often whizzed past the nose of the devoted "balloon-tugger," but in time we began to accept these statements with a good deal of reserve, realising that they were intended to emphasise the need for care on our part.

During the whole of this time we were flying under ideal conditions and with some of the finest pilots in the service. The days were long and, for the most part, sunny. On only two or three occasions was there any considerable wind. We generally flew without special flying clothing.

When not on the aerodrome we played tennis, or bathed, or idled about in the grounds of the spacious hotel which had been taken over by the school. There were theatres, concerts, cricket matches, golf. It was a period of strenuous work and delightful relaxation. Once or twice, when the wind blew from the north-east, we could hear the dull reverberations of the guns in Flanders. But, although most of us had come from "over there," we contrived for the nonce to forget the war. We lived in, and for, the present; frankly, passionately; knowing that sooner or later the all-embracing tentacles of the war-machine would stretch out, embrace us, and tear us away from this happy dalliance.

Mac retained his advantage, passed his flying tests ahead of me, and was posted to a Bristol Fighter squadron in France. Just before I said "good-bye" to him he asked me to try to follow him to the same squadron. When the time came for me to leave the school of aerial gunnery, however, I was willy-nilly sent to a home-defence night-flying squadron. I wrote Mac telling him of what I then considered my bad luck. But I have always been a believer in Kismet, and I

A "Zeppelin" Patrol

settled down to my new work hoping that the fortunes of war would bring us together again. Then came the Great Silence. Mac had given his life for England. I did not hear the story until many months afterwards, and then—the first shock over—I gloried in his triumph. *Per Ardua ad Astra.*

I shall always remember my first flight by night. Curiously enough, it was during one of the earlier Zeppelin raids on London and the Eastern Counties.

The moon was on the wane, and we were flying at about three thousand feet, when I saw quite plainly shrapnel bursting in the air several miles to the south. We made in the direction of the firing, climbing steadily the whole time, but saw no hostile aircraft. We were following the coast; the sea looked wonderfully mysterious in the shine of the moon. All round the horizon was a dim curtain of mist. It was as if one swam in a vast circular bath of clear water, the rim of the bath being vague and far away, and made of a kind of cloudy grey marble.

We saw flashes to the south—shrapnel, star-shells, and parachute flares. But we had arrived at the limit of our patrol area without having seen anything of the enemy aircraft, and had therefore to return. Nosing northwards, we gradually lost height, and then flew low over sand-dunes and swamps and marshy fields to our aerodrome.

Landing a machine at night is no superlatively easy matter. In certain weather conditions it is difficult to gauge with any certainty whether the machine is a hundred feet or only a few feet above ground level. Sometimes when you are just coming into the petrol or electric flares which are placed on all night-flying aerodromes for landing purposes, and are preparing to "flatten out," you discover that you have either underestimated or overshot the aerodrome. This means that you have to put on your engine again, go round once more and have another shot for it. On this night, however, we touched ground by the first flare, pulled up after a very short run, and taxied easily over to the hangars.

CHAPTER IV

"CRASHED"

MY log-book shows that for a week after my arrival at the night-flying squadron I practised bomb-dropping by day and night in all kinds of weather, into and with the wind, and from all heights up to two thousand five hundred feet. In the centre of the aerodrome a large circle had been painted in chalk; an "O.K." consisted in dropping the bomb so that it fell anywhere within this circle. At night the target was a parallelogram, the corners of which were marked by flaring hurricane lamps.

After a week's constant practice most of us became fairly proficient in the art of bomb-dropping. Sometimes one or other of us would be deputed to stand out on the aerodrome and "mark" for another observer who was doing his tests. This was a rather trying job. We used to call it "death dodging." You would take your scoring-card with its bull's-eye and concentric circles marked upon it, and proceed to a spot as near to, or as far from, the target as your temperament dictated. Some fellows would stand in the geometric centre of the ring and allege that they felt safer there; others would hang about near the edge of the field, and with the fall of each bomb would dash forward, measure roughly its distance from the bull's-eye, then retreat once more to the comparative security of the hedge.

In daylight you would watch the machine approach the target in a long straight glide, the observer leaning over the front of the nacelle, his eyes glued on his bomb-sight, his right arm uplifted in readiness to give the signal to his pilot. If you were keen-sighted you would see him drop his hand, and at the same instant the bomb would leave the rack and commence its downward journey. That was the time—in the words of our Flight-Commander—to "keep your eyes skinned." For the first three or four seconds you could generally follow the bomb in its flight; after that you heard a rapidly increasing whistle, then a thud, followed by a cloud of earth, grass roots and small stones.

The bombs employed were dummy fifteen-pounders—practically the same bombs as those used in France, but minus charge and detonator. They always hit the earth with a sound which can only be described in words as a "concentrated wonk," and generally buried themselves several inches in the ground. At the end of each practice a fatigue party would dig them out with pick and shovel.

The duty of the marker was to decide how near or how far the bombs were from the centre of the chalk ring. The orders were that only one bomb at a time was to be released; but sometimes, from some cause which was never explained, two missiles would come down singing a simultaneous song of warning to the marker below. And then it behoved that harassed individual to make himself scarce. It is neither pleasant nor profitable to "stop" a projectile composed of a carcass of tin-plate weighing fifteen pounds and hurtling through space at the rate of over two hundred and fifty miles an hour.

After the release of each bomb the machine had to make a wide circuit of the aerodrome in order to allow the marker time to "measure up" the preceding shot; then it would come gliding down upon you again; once more you would intently watch its course and wait anxiously for the observer's signal to his pilot.

At night-time the terrors of marking were intensified. The same type of bomb was used, but its vitals were charged with a compound of magnesium which caused it to burst into flames upon impact with the ground. I remember one intensely dark night when a new observer released a bomb too late; we heard it whistling its merry earthward course, and, instinctively realising that it would meet the ground at a point too near us to be comfortable, we dived underneath a three-ton lorry near which we happened to be standing. A second or two later the bomb burst into flames within a couple of yards of the lorry, and the blazing magnesium scorched the heel of my boot as I lay on the ground.

Several months later I visited my old training squadron and discovered that bomb-proof dug-outs had been built near each target. No longer has marking any terrors; on the contrary, it is a "light duty" job.

The day came at last when I had once more to leave "England, home and beauty" and proceed overseas for active service. Curiously enough my last flight in England provided me with my first "crash." A new pilot had arrived at the squadron, and I had been detailed to show him round the country. We left the aerodrome about eleven o'clock in the morning, flew over a neighbouring town to the coast, then along the coast for some distance, and so home. We arrived over the aerodrome again at about fifteen hundred feet. Suddenly, without any warning whatever, the pilot switched off his engine, pulled his stick right back, and "stalled" the machine. She first slid back on her tail, then flopped over, got her nose down vertically, and began to spin. I gripped the sides of the nacelle, shut my eyes, and waited for the end. But it was not to be. The pilot pulled her out at about five hundred feet and made an exceptionally good landing.

This was the first time I had been spun on an F.E. machine, but the pilot seemed to know all about it, and I regained my confidence in him when he told me proudly that in private life he was a trick cyclist. I argued that a man who could negotiate a bicycle across a tight-rope could be trusted to spin an F.E. without smashing either it or its occupants. I therefore had no trepidation in going up with him again that evening on a short moonlight reconnaissance.

We took off the aerodrome in great style, our engine was running sweetly, and I settled down to enjoy my last " flip " in England. I knew the country well, and it was no effort to put my trickcyclist right when he showed any tendency to wander from our given route.

The night was warm and subtly sensuous. The moonshine, delicate behind lofty cirrus clouds, softened the outlines of things, made them vague and indefinite. We could see the rivers, silver ribbons winding down to a silver sea. And the fens were great lakes of molten silver. All water was silver, and woodlands were little black blobs on silver shields, and there were no houses or works of man to spoil the breadth and the width of nature.

For two hours we flew through an aerial fairyland. I sat in the nacelle and gave full rein to my imagination.

I was awakened rudely from my dream. There came a sudden cessation of all sound. I missed the steady, monotonous thunder of the engine.

"Crashed"

The machine shuddered and quivered on her stalling point, her nose went up, her tail slid back into the abyss. We lost a thousand feet of height in less than five seconds. As our nose dropped over there was an intense glare of light behind me. We were spinning down now, a steep, narrow spin on our axis, and the fierce blaze made me believe that we were on fire. Down below, a thousand feet or so, I saw the landing-flares of an aerodrome coming up to meet us with alarming rapidity.

After a time the glare died away, and I realised that my pilot had inadvertently switched on his Holt flares—electric-magnesium lights fixed under each lower wing-tip to assist one to land in bad weather.

We did several spins to the right, pulled out, then reversed badly, hung for a second poised in mid-air, booms and spars and fabric trembling with the sudden reaction, then flopped over once more and span to the left, rapidly, violently. I realised, almost without emotion, that the pilot had lost control, and that we were going to crash badly. It came to me in a flash, and I hoped only that it would be quick and merciful.

Beneath us was a rapidly revolving kaleidoscope of lights. I was unable now to distinguish the landing-flares from the lights in tents and hangars; there was nothing but a vague, confused shimmer, something like the subdued glare of a blast furnace with the lid on.

Then we were down. The machine stabilised herself, but came out of the spin too violently, and before the pilot could regain control we touched ground on one wheel, across the wind, and at a rate of at least one hundred miles an hour.

There was a cracking and splintering of spars and booms, a thud as the engine nosed into the ground, and then silence.

I crept gingerly out of the debris, the pilot followed, and we both produced cigarette-cases. " I'll never spin an F.E. at night-time again," he said. " I'd sooner bike across the Straits of Dover on a tight-rope."

CHAPTER V

FIRST " FLIPS " IN FRANCE

THE morning was yet young as our car raced along the broad white road, and we felt that it was good to be alive. There were three of us— all observers—and we had been posted to one of the finest night-flying squadrons on the Western Front. We had trained together at the same gunnery school in England, had been taken for our first " flips " on the same antiquated school " bus," finally had served together in the same home-defence squadron. Now we were coming out to France together to fly on active service.

We had landed in France late one wintry afternoon, and proceeded that same night to a large town in Flanders. Next morning a car was sent down from the aerodrome, and we raced along the straight, broad *route nationale* to the scene of our future activities.

On arrival at the aerodrome we discovered that we already knew many of the pilots and observers in the squadron, and several of them tried to "put the wind up" us by relating hair-raising accounts of the narrow shaves they had had while flying over the lines. But we soon settled down to learn our jobs, study the maps, memorise the lighthouses, and get accustomed to the general ideas of service flying.

They broke us in gradually. On the second day I had a "flip" round the aerodrome to get the "hang" of the country; on the third day I flew over to a neighbouring aerodrome for lunch; and a few days later I did a practice daylight reconnaissance along the Ypres sector.

The sun was shining as we got into our "bus," and all the world seemed gay. My pilot was in great form. We climbed well and, at about three thousand feet, headed for Ypres. As we got nearer to the trenches the roads became more and more congested with troops and moving columns of supplies.

Looking over the side of the "bus" I could see the tiny khaki-clad figures marching in fours along all the roads to the line, and I thought of the days when I walked along these selfsame roads with many a dear fellow who has since crossed the Great Divide.

We passed over Ypres at under a thousand feet. For miles around in every direction the ground was pocked with shell-holes. I believe that in all the world you cannot find a more tragic panorama of destruction than in the land round "Wipers." I have been down on the Somme, have seen Pozières, Grandcourt, Beaumont-Hamel, have gazed at the ghosts of Bapaume and Arras; but nothing has moved me quite so much as these heroic remnants of Ypres seen from the air that sunny winter morning.

The gunners were putting down a barrage on the Passchendaele Ridge; I could see the spurts of flame beneath, and away in the east regular lines of shell-bursts. There was also a fire of considerable magnitude some distance behind the German lines, and far above our heads, at eight thousand feet or more, a formation of British scout machines was dodging "archie." I realised that I was again "at the war."

We turned southwards, passing over historic battlefields—Hill 60, Messines, Armentières—and so back to our aerodrome, where we arrived in time to witness from the air the last five minutes of a football match.

Later in the evening the barometer went down with a crash, heavy banks of storm clouds swept up out of the east, and by the time we went to bed that night it was snowing heavily and blowing more than half a gale.

For three days we did no flying. Then the wind died down, and I was detailed for another "flip" up to the lines, this time covering the Arras sector. It was with the same pilot and in the same machine as before. The snow was on the ground, and we needed, therefore, a slightly longer run before we "took off."

We climbed gently away from the aerodrome. Roads and railways were visible as long black lines across the snow; rivers and canals were difficult to see, as most of them were frozen over, and there was nothing to break the continuity of the snow-level; forests were seen as great black blobs in vast white frames of snow.

We flew the whole way parallel to the lines. There seemed to be little or no activity until we got near Lens, which was being desultorily shelled. The Vimy Ridge presented a vastly different aspect

First "Flips" in France

from what it did when I was there in the days of the "push." Where formerly had been a maze of trenches, lines of barbed wire, shell-craters, the desolation and solitude of No Man's Land, were now whole colonies of " tin " huts, tents, canteens, cinema theatres, and all the accessories of camp and billet life a few miles behind the lines.

I had never seen Arras from the air; still, the dear old place seemed to be strangely familiar, and I picked out many a landmark of the past. We flew over the town at a couple of thousand feet, then "tootled off" to the line, or as near to it as we were allowed to go. An inquisitive artillery observation machine hung on to our tail for several minutes. He was evidently much perturbed as to our identity. The probability is that he had never seen our type of night-bomber before. We shook the fellow off eventually, however, and I had a good look at the sector in which I had done the most of my trench campaigning. Then we "beetled" off for home and tea, arriving at the aerodrome a little before dusk.

I now began to feel that I was something of a flying veteran. I had had my practice "flips." My next show was to be a bombing raid over the lines.

CHAPTER VI

MY FIRST BOMBING RAID

At midnight the sky was filled with storm clouds. A "show" seemed out of the question, and we all went to bed. But at three o'clock in the morning whistles were blowing, flares were being put out, sleepy men were opening the hangars, and orderlies were running round the camp warning pilots and observers to prepare for a "stunt."

The sky had cleared, and there was practically no wind. At half-past three that morning the first machine took the air.

My pilot and I were second off the ground. Our engine was running perfectly, we climbed rapidly, and in less than a quarter of an hour we glimpsed ahead of us the great arc of gun-flashes which represented the buttress against which the two hostile armed forces of Europe were hammering.

A few minutes later we passed the last of the

My First Bombing Raid

lighthouses, switched off all our lights, throttled back our engine, and approached the battle zone.

Below us, as we flew over the trenches, we could see the spurts of rifle and machine-gun fire, the firing of batteries, the bursts of shells and grenades, long lines of coloured Verey lights stretching away north and south as far as the eye could reach. It was amazing to think that down there, three thousand feet and more beneath us, tens of thousands of human beings in trenches and saps and dug-outs were busily engaged in the great game of war.

Our operation orders that night were for one of the most distant Gotha aerodromes in Belgium. To reach our objective we had to negotiate not only the usual " hate " which one more or less expects over the enemy's lines and reserve positions, but also the powerful defences of three large towns which lay between us and the target we were attacking.

To my surprise, however, we got practically no " hate " over the lines, probably owing to the fact that the enemy was too busy dealing with our gun-barrages to pay much attention to us. On quiet nights, when there was little or no activity, as soon as they heard the drone of our engines the long searchlights stabbed the sky and the "archies" greeted us with vigorous "woufs" and bangs. On this night, however, only one enterprising "onion" battery had a burst at us, while about a dozen tracer machine-gun bullets came up from the Boche trenches.

Visibility was perfect, and we could see Lille with ease before we got to it—a black, tentacled blob in the encircling fields of snow. We flew over the Menin Road, and I thought of the times I had passed along it in those far-off infantry days. Near here an "archie" battery violently "hated" us, while six or seven searchlights picked us up, and we had to dive and side-slip several times in order to get out of their beams.

Near Courtrai we ran into a bank of dense black mist, and in order to see anything my pilot dived the machine. At five hundred feet above the ground we came suddenly out of the clouds. In the meantime I had lost my bearings, but fortunately was able to pick up a railway line with a double set of metals running due east.

I identified this on my map, and for some time we followed it. Then we picked up the road

My First Bombing Raid

which went down to our objective, and about half an hour later we found ourselves, with our engine throttled down, over one of the largest Gotha aerodromes in Belgium.

Everything was quiet. Below us we could see their hangars, workshops and hutments revealed clearly in the strong glare of the moon. I wondered at the amazing quietness, yet had an uneasy feeling that those grey-coated fellows down below were waiting for us. We flew round in wide circles, gradually losing height and with our engine just "ticking over." Away to the north I saw shrapnel bursting in the sky, and I knew then that a machine of one of our other squadrons had also arrived at its objective.

We got down to a thousand feet before we commenced our long glide on to the target. At five hundred feet I pulled my bomb levers, then glued my eyes on the ground waiting for the detonations. The first bomb burst—a dull red flash and a report like a siege-gun—in the middle of a group of sheds, and almost immediately the German anti-aircraft defences opened up. "archies," "flaming onions," machine-gun bullets were hurled up at us; the whole firmament seemed filled with groping, menacing fingers of light. I fired my gun until most of my ammunition had gone, and then, having stirred up such vast "chunks of hate" that we deemed it unhealthy to remain over the aerodrome any longer, we put our nose once more west and made off for home.

Over Menin, at six o'clock that morning, we ran into another "archie" barrage, and for about twenty seconds the whole machine, quite out of control, rocked and quivered violently, then "carried on." A few minutes later, just as a wintry dawn was breaking, we recrossed the lines.

CHAPTER VII

TESTING THE WEATHER

"THE following pilots and observers will report in the Operation-Room to-day at 5 p.m." This was the formal summons, followed by a long list of names, which an orderly read out in the mess every day just before tea-time. If you didn't happen to be in the mess at the time, your Flight-Commander, when he met you, would tell you casually, "Map-Room at five o'clock, old boy. You're down to fly with So-and-so."

"What's the target, old man?" you would ask.

"Oh, the aerodrome at X," or "The sidings at Y," or "Billets near Z," he would reply.

You took a glance at the sky—all flying men become in time very reliable judges of the weather —and then you walked across to the hangars and had a look at your machine. If you are an observer you are responsible for the reliability of all the apparatus you use during operations—your guns, maps, lights, compasses, and bomb-controls. You get your gun and test it in the gun-pit; you make sure that your maps are in position and that the reading lights are in order; you try the working of your bomb-racks and control levers; and periodically you get the compass officer to swing and correct all the compasses on the machine.

If you are a pilot you will have run your engine up earlier in the day and have taken your " bus " for a test flip. On these occasions, unless your observer is particularly anxious to have a joy ride, you carry as passenger the corporal-fitter, who, as your chief mechanic, is responsible for your engine. He listens to the sound of it while in the air, and on reaching the ground again remedies any faults which may been detected. Your life and the life of your observer depend upon the work and the ceaseless attention of your fitter, your rigger, and the mechanics under them; and, taking them as a whole, they are a wonderful crowd of fellows, these air-mechanics.

Your machine is reported " serviceable," guns and ammunition are aboard, her racks are loaded

Testing the Weather

with bombs, everything is ready for the night's "show."

In the Map-Room the C.O. officially gives you your target, says a few quiet words, and you settle down to study your maps and discuss alternative routes with your pilot.

On the night following my first raid over the lines the weather was too treacherous for any attempt at long-distance bombing. Showers of sleet fell at intervals; the ground was shrouded in a dank mist; and heavy banks of clouds scurried across the face of the moon.

My pilot and I, however, were ordered up in a wireless machine to test atmospheric conditions more intimately, and to report on the possibilities of a short "show." The surface of the aerodrome was in a wretched condition. Its composition resembled a mixture of half-frozen glue, and my pilot, after an inordinately long run, had to "yank" the "bus" off the ground, barely clearing the telegraph wires at the farther end of the aerodrome.

At about a thousand feet the ground became quite invisible; the only things one could see were lights blinking through the mist.

We flew twice round the aerodrome, testing our wireless installation; then, on intimation from the ground that they were receiving our signals clearly, we took a rough compass-course to one of the lighthouses. During the whole of our flight we were able to remain in touch with the aerodrome, and every two or three minutes we wired down a weather report. It was distinctly amusing to reflect that at these identical moments, somewhere within twenty or thirty miles of us, a German night-flying pilot was probably sending down to his squadron office similar messages to ours. We often heard the Boche reports, and they doubtless often heard ours, so that, at any rate, we knew each other's opinion of the weather.

As we neared the line that night the conditions became worse. Twice we encountered heavy showers of rain. Navigating entirely by compass and lights, we wandered down to Bethune, and in the neighbourhood of the La Bassée Canal witnessed a fierce gun duel. We were flying fairly low, and the intense white flames of the guns seemed to stab the fog violently.

German shells were bursting in our lines, and we could see away over the canal a long, straggling ribbon of dull red flashes. That was our barrage methodically pounding the German trenches. Directly beneath us, alternately blazing up and away, a big fire burned fiercely.

Realising that the weather was rapidly becoming " dangerous" we decided to return to the aerodrome. On the way back we ran into a rainstorm of such severity that I had to crouch low in my seat to avoid being blinded. The pilot, behind his wind-screen, was able more effectively to protect his eyes, but he confessed later that he felt as though he was "driving through a solid wall of water," and that he "hadn't the least notion where he was, or whether the machine was flying on an even keel." He could hear the roar of his engine, and concentrated as far as possible on keeping the "bus" in the air until we should have passed through the bank of rain.

Then quite suddenly we experienced a vast relief. No longer did the rain lash and beat about us, stinging and torturing our skin. We had flown through it. A patch of clear sky showed above, and three or four miles ahead we could see aerodrome lights. The landing flares were lit, and they were sending up rockets to guide us in. Under difficult conditions we made a " clean " landing, and, on recounting our experience in the squadron office, the " show " for that night was " washed out."

CHAPTER VIII

THE LUCK OF "LIGHTHOUSE LUKE"

MY log-book shows that a week's "dud" flying weather followed, a week of relaxation—lectures in the morning, long walks in the afternoon, cards and music in the evening. During all this time I was gradually becoming acquainted with the history and traditions of the squadron, and I soon discovered that we had amongst us some of the cleverest and most experienced night-pilots in the world.

I am going to tell you a tale of one of them.

We call him "Lighthouse Luke," a term of endearment which is no reflection on his abilities as a pilot. It is now pretty generally known that in certain kinds of weather night-flyers find their way about largely with the aid of ground lights; and the term "Lighthouse Luke"—spoken in jest one night in the mess—would seem to impute to its owner a fondness for flying round and round the lighthouses instead of crossing the lines and doing his job. Needless to say, this is not the case. No pilot in the squadron has done better work than old "Lighthouse Luke," and I am sure that if he reads these lines he will pardon this little joke at his expense.

We are a high-spirited crowd of fellows. We love a little friendly badinage, and no one more so than "Lighthouse Luke" himself. We recognised his gifts as a humorist before he had been with the squadron a week, and his first show over the lines was probably the most pricelessly humorous thing he will ever do, even if he lives to be a hundred. To begin with, he is the owner of the most ludicrous flying-boots in all the world. Charlie Chaplin is nowhere in it compared with "Lighthouse Luke" dressed up for a "show." The feet of these boots are about nine inches too long, and they have been trodden down on each side so that, as dear old "Lighthouse" toddles out to his machine, his legs bend gracefully outwards and inwards, and remind one of a goose on the day before a certain part of its anatomy is manufactured into *pâté de foie gras*.

The night of Luke's first show was dark and "dud," and, as he was being gently assisted into

The Luck of "Lighthouse Luke"

his "bus" by his admiring mechanics, he was heard to mutter, "Ha, ha! 'Tis duddy dark!" He got off the ground in great style, but nothing more was heard of him until the fragments of his machine arrived back next morning on a three-ton lorry. His observer was sent down to the South of France to recuperate. But old "Lighthouse Luke" turned up, smiling, complete with flying-boots and the remains of the deceased "bus."

The story is this. He had dropped his "pills" on a railway station in Hunland, then putting his nose west, he "beetled off" for our own lines. After that he remembered little except that it got so dark that he could see nothing whatever outside his "office." He came down lower in the hope of recognising some feature on the ground.

Then suddenly he hit a railway embankment, the under-carriage fell into a ditch, the rest of his machine sat down across the rails.

A dark object hurtled through the air and landed in some soft mud about fifty yards away. "That," said "Lighthouse Luke" laconically, "was my observer. Then I picked myself up out of the ruins and noticed, to my horror, that a train was approaching in the distance. I ran along the metals to the nearest signal-post, shinned up it, and stopped the train. When I returned, a crowd of angry Frenchmen were standing round my machine demanding why I had chosen the railway to land on."

When a machine crashes, a salvaging party is generally sent out to " take it down," the wires being carefully unscrewed, instruments packed up, and the engine, ailerons, and other important parts rescued, to be patched up and used again.

Poor old Luke's " bus," however, was destined for a more ignominious end.

" Those energetic Frenchmen," he said plaintively, " attacked it with hatchets and crowbars, smashing through tail-booms, spars, and wings as if they had been so much firewood. It was painful to see them throw all the bits, as soon as they had chopped them up, into the field where my observer was still lying. Then a great crane arrived miraculously, picked my engine up and chucked it contemptuously beside the rest of the wreckage. Finally, they bent back the bulged rails, and the delayed train rolled past. Their railway communications restored, they all became amiable once more, took us to an inn, gave us coffee and cognac,

The Luck of "Lighthouse Luke"

and even thanked me volubly for having saved their train.

"Next morning I left my observer in the nearest hospital, piled what remained of the ill-fated 'bus' on to the lorry which had been sent out, and came home."

Dear old "Lighthouse" is still "carrying on." He has done some brilliant work—but he has smashed no more French railways.

CHAPTER IX

ON WINGS OF HAPPY CHANCE

A FEW days before the battle of Cambrai we received sudden orders to move from our aerodrome. On an afternoon of scurrying storm clouds the whole squadron flew south to an advanced landing-ground opposite the Cambrai front, and some three or four miles only from the first line of trenches. There were no available hangars, and during the whole of that battle our machines remained in the open; we ourselves slept in them, or under them, or on the floors of the few "tin" huts which we found there, or in any odd corners where we could get out of the wind and rain. It proved to be that period of my service in the Flying Corps which most approximated to my experiences in the trenches.

Notwithstanding all the discomfort of it, however, we carried out some very interesting and exciting raids. Due east of the landing-ground, and some seven or eight miles away from it, was a

On Wings of Happy Chance

long, straggling village cut in two by a canal. That part of the village east of the canal was in German hands; British troops held the western end of the village as far as the canal bank.

Our orders were to bomb—and bomb continuously from dusk to dawn—the part of the village still in German occupation, in which concentrations of troops for a counter-attack had been reported the afternoon before.

Another night-flying squadron had joined forces with us. We took the air as soon as it became dark enough to camouflage our machines, and, using as few lights as possible, flew across the lines in twos and threes and little bunches, laid our "eggs," and returned to our starting-point for more ammunition and bombs. We all flew low that night, partly because it was scarcely worth climbing to any height on such a short journey, and partly because, in order not to endanger the lives of our own fellows in the trenches, we had been ordered to take particular care that we were over the canal before releasing our bombs or firing our guns.

It was an amazing spectacle. The moon, shining fitfully through scudding wracks of clouds, was nearly at the full. The air between the aerodrome and the target seemed to be one long lane of British machines. On the way home we met a dozen or more machines going out; on the way out we met the same number returning home. We blinked our navigation lights at each other and went on with the work.

As all the world knows, the later stages of the battle of Cambrai were fought in storms of wind and rain. It was dangerous flying weather, but we felt that the fellows in the trenches needed our help; and to this day we like to think—as the Corps Commander subsequently told us—that our persistent bombing of the enemy's concentrations assisted very materially in breaking up several counter-attacks.

We did not get through this trying period without several accidents. One pilot had his petrol tank shot through, but got home safely. When just over the aerodrome his engine burst into flames. He chose the quickest way of getting down to the ground—side-slipping—and made a good, if somewhat fast, landing. Both he and his observer were unhurt. The flames of the burning engine had been quenched in the last rapid dive to earth.

On Wings of Happy Chance

Another pilot brought off a wonderful forced landing in a snowstorm within a mile of the line. His engine had "cut out" altogether, and he glided down quite blindly. Through the driving snow he could scarcely see ten yards in any direction. Suddenly he glimpsed the ground immediately beneath the wheels of his under-carriage, jerked the stick back mechanically and "flattened out." When eventually he pulled up he discovered that the nose of his machine was within two yards of an enormous shell-crater. One second more and they would have gone into it, and that meant certain death.

Another of my friends was hit in the head and shoulder while flying at eight hundred feet over Douai. He flopped forward over the joy-stick, and the "bus" immediately nosed earthwards. His observer, realising that something had gone wrong, leaned over from the front seat, pushed the pilot off the stick, and pulled the machine out of her dive just in time. The pilot had fainted. With one hand the observer held the unconscious man back in his seat; with the other he kept the joy-stick straight, the machine climbing steadily. He had his back to the course they were flying, and his main object was to get the machine over the lines, then crash her, and trust to luck. He had little or no lateral control, because he could not touch the rudder, and it was a very dark night. However, with full control of his throttle and elevator, there was not much danger of side-slipping, because the machine was stable, and, provided she was not banked at too steep an angle, would take up her own rudder.

Every now and then his right arm would become cramped with the strain of keeping the pilot in his seat. He would change hands, watching his instruments grimly. The pilot would again flop forward, to be pressed back with the left hand, while the tired right hand grabbed the stick and rescued the machine from her dive.

For more than half an hour my friend managed to keep up this sort of pump-handling, and then, to his intense joy, he saw beneath him the long line of Verey lights over the trenches. He flew for another two or three minutes, then "throttled back," and shook the unconscious figure in the pilot's seat.

"Look here, old boy," he shouted, as the pilot opened his eyes, "I've flown the 'bus' over the

On Wings of Happy Chance

lines. It's *your* job now. Can you land her?"
The pilot responded to the appeal and "flattened
out" in time to "write off" the "bus" in a shell-
hole. But they "got away with it." Friendly
Portuguese officers gave the observer fried steak
and "pukka" port, and sent the wounded pilot
back to hospital through one of their own clearing-
stations.

On another occasion one of our machines was
seven miles over the lines on a pitch-black night.
The engine cut out completely. The pilot tried
all the usual dodges—diving steeply, turning the
self-starter, switching over to service tank. But
nothing happened.

"We're for it!" he shouted to his observer.
"Unscrew your gun!"

A machine-gun was firing viciously from the
ground, and they were less than the length of a
football field from it, when, with a sudden roar,
the engine "opened out." All the way home she
gave trouble—spitting and spluttering like a Manx
cat—but they managed to make our lines and land
in a field without breaking anything.

On the following night an observer's handker-
chief blew back into the engine and choked it, and

we heard the machine miles away from the aerodrome clanking home on about two cylinders. He had to glide the final four miles, absolutely without engine. Fortunately, there was a stiff following wind, and he got in easily.

A " dud " engine, an essential " control " shot away, a bad wound causing the pilot temporarily to lose consciousness—these three factors have been responsible for some of the most amazing escapes from death in the chronicles of war. These few little accidents which happened to pilots in our squadron during the Cambrai fighting are only some of the very many cases I know of where fortune has waited upon pluck, and brought many a dear, good fellow back to safety when all the odds seemed to be against him.

After ten days' strenuous and difficult flying—in snow, rain, and heavy winds, through fog and clouds—we got the order to return to our aerodrome. We flew back with warped wings and slackened wires, with ailerons and elevators curled by long days' and nights' exposure to the elements, with " sloppy " controls, damp magnetos, engines that coughed and spat, machines that were nose-heavy and tail-heavy, that flew " right-wing low "

On Wings of Happy Chance

and "left-wing low." In short, there was not a "bus" in the squadron which did not urgently need a rest and a thorough overhaul. My own pilot conjugated the general situation as follows:

"Engines—*dud*; rigging—*dudder*; pilots and observers—*duddest*."

In the days which followed I spoke with many of the infantrymen and gunners who had been through the Cambrai push, and they all agreed that it was great "to hear the mighty hum of our machines as we flew over their lines." Many of them, from points of vantage, had seen the savage little bursts of flame from our Lewis guns as we searched the roads for German troops; nearly always they were able to hear the detonations of our bombs.

The knowledge that on such occasions as these our work in the air was of *direct and immediate* advantage to our comrades in the trenches made all the peril and the gamble of the game worth while.

CHAPTER X

OUR COMIC CRASH

About three weeks before Christmas the weather cleared, and the squadron carried out some very successful raids. Ill-fortune dogged my footsteps, however, and I began to be looked upon as a " Jinks "—that is, a man who brings bad luck to a machine. It didn't matter what machine I went up in, something happened—either the petrol system gave up the ghost, or the water-jacket burst, or tappet rods broke mysteriously, or the oil pump expired, or the pressure went " dud."

Once we started on a raid in high hopes this time of " getting there." The engine seemed to be running perfectly, yet we had only just crossed the lines when the pressure gave out altogether. My pilot switched over to his gravity tank and pumped the pressure up again. Then he tried the main tank once more, but again the pressure went and the engine " conked." Finally, he decided that as we were on a long show it would be madness

Our Comic Crash

to go any farther with such a dud engine. We therefore brought the "bus" round, and came home on our reserve tank.

On the following night, when some two or three miles over the line, our temperature suddenly went up, and after a few preliminary coughs the engine cut out altogether.

"We've been hit!" my pilot shouted through the telephone which connected our seats. "I think it's a machine-gun bullet through the radiator. Water run out! Engine red hot! We'll have to come down, old boy! I'll try and make the lines. Get your Verey pistol ready. I'll drop the parachute flare when we're over." I cleared my "office" for action—that is, got the gun off its mounting and laid it on the floor, so that if I were thrown out in the crash it would not hit me. There was not enough time to worry, but I remember vaguely wondering whether we should land in a shell-hole or on the top of a house or into the edge of a wood.

Fortunately we had a pretty stiff wind behind us. Had it been against us we could not possibly have made the lines. As it was, we crossed the trenches at about a thousand feet, losing height rapidly. The parachute flare refused to burn, and I therefore fired a succession of Verey lights. The night was dark, but the lights showed us roughly the nature of the country we were flying over. We glided down across a small town, and then, in the flickering glare of one of my rockets, we glimpsed what looked like a long, flat field.

"Landing there!" shouted my pilot, pointing frantically at the field. "Get ready for the bump, old boy!"

We flew down the field with the wind behind us, the while I glued my eyes on to the ground searching for obstacles. A tree-stump, a fence, a ditch, some telegraph wires might spell the difference between life and death. But everything seemed to be clear.

We turned back into the wind, in order that when we touched the ground we should have it dead against us, thus shortening our run and minimising the chances of disaster. The pilot switched on his landing lights, which enabled us to see some fifteen or twenty yards ahead. I noticed that the grass was rather long. Then, just as I imagined all danger to be past, a row of tall trees loomed ahead. Our speed at that moment was between fifty and

Our Comic Crash

sixty miles an hour, and impact with the trees at that velocity would mean certain destruction both for ourselves and the machine. My pilot did the only thing possible. He put his joy-stick right forward, the nose of the machine went down, and we gained speed suddenly. Then he pulled the stick almost back into his stomach. With the additional flying speed he had gained by the slight dive he was able to "zoom" over the trees and "pancake" into a ploughed field on the other side.

The under-carriage was swept off altogether, but we were on the ground once more, unhurt, and within sound of British rifle and machine-gun fire. Our bombs had buried themselves, on the impact, in about six inches of gravelly furrow; the engine, which we examined in the light of a hand torch, was a mass of white metal, due to its having "seized-up" after the water in the radiator had all run out; but otherwise not a plane had been damaged, not a wire strained. These, together with the booms and instruments, were salvaged under fire the next day, but the engine and under-carriage had to be "written off."

On that same night two other of our machines had forced landings. There followed a period of engine trouble for the whole squadron. This was almost entirely due to the intense cold. Water froze in the radiators. Two engines " seized-up " while being tested on the ground. Innumerable tail-skids were broken every day by machines landing on ground frozen hard as steel, then unavoidably skidding and slewing round so violently that *something* had to go.

During this bitter month the squadron had more engine trouble and forced landings than during any other period of its history. Every night those of us who were back safely would stand on the aerodrome waiting for some machine which was overdue. " Who's not down? " we would ask.

" Oh! it's Bobby to-night," or " Daylight Dave," or " Piccadilly Percy," as the case might be.

Then we would strain our eyes eastward. Yes, there was still hope. We could see strings of " flaming onions " all round the horizon; German searchlights still probed the sky. Evidently some British machines had not yet regained our lines. Then we would see the navigation lights of a machine in the distance; her engine, throbbing

Our Comic Crash

through the night sky, would become more and more audible.

"This must be Bobby," we would say. But she would pass over us to another aerodrome.

"Oh, that is one of So-and-so's machines. They had a more distant target than ours," someone would inform us.

Sometimes three machines would come along together, and not one of them land. Then the recording officer would stroll out and say:

"It's all right, you fellows! You can 'wash-out.' No more 'shows' to-night. Weather coming up 'dud.' Bobby's down at X——. 'The Flappers' Ruin' landed at No. 5. Everybody accounted for!"

Then we would go into the mess, and for two or three jolly hours we would forget that such a thing as an aeroplane existed.

The amazing fact about this trying period, however, is that during the whole of the time not one pilot or observer sustained more than a bruise as the result of all our forced landings. Machines came down, landed in shell-holes and ditches, smashed trees and telegraph wires, turned upside down, were broken to pieces, yet every time their occupants were thrown clear or emerged from the ruins with nothing more than a mouthful of French soil, a scratched wrist, a bruised posterior.

My own run of bad luck culminated in what might almost be termed a "comic" crash. A new pilot had arrived in the squadron to take over the duties of Flight-Commander. He had done a great deal of night flying in France, was a man of vast experience on the type of machine we were flying, and later proved to be one of our most successful pilots. I was detailed one windy afternoon to fly with him on a short test reconnaissance of the country round about the aerodrome.

We ran the engine up, taxied out to the farthest corner of the aerodrome, got our nose into the wind, then, opening the throttle, moved off down the aerodrome with ever-increasing speed. The pilot got the tail of the machine up, but held her nose down, so that we were flying at about eighty or ninety miles an hour, while still just skimming the ground. His object was to pull the stick back suddenly, then "zoom" out of the aerodrome. But he kept his stick forward a second too long. The under-carriage hit the village pump with a sound like the report of a big gun.

Our Comic Crash

The next thing I remember is that we were heading for some telegraph wires, oscillating violently from side to side. Instinctively I ducked my head, preferring to be badly hurt on the ground than decapitated in the air. But the pilot, with amazing coolness, dived under the wires, swung the " bus " on to her wing-tip in order to avoid colliding with one of the telegraph poles, then put her down as gently as if nothing had happened.

By all the rules of flying we should both have been killed that afternoon. On impact with the pump the machine should have nosed into the ground, in which case we should have had the engine on the top of us, and could not have hoped to "get away" with our lives.

That crash broke my run of bad luck, and during the ensuing three months I was able to take part in every raid carried out by the squadron.

CHAPTER XI

WE GET A NEW MACHINE

ON the day following our crash my pilot and I were sent down to one of the big aircraft depots to " collect " a new experimental machine which had been specially fitted with a small gun firing two-pounder shells. We motored along the snow-covered roads in one of the wing cars, accompanied by our gunnery officer, who was interested in the new weapon and had promised that ours should be the first machine to use it over the lines. Our road led through Lillers and Doullens down to the old Somme country over which I had fought in the winter of 1916 and the spring of 1917, and over which I was soon to fly night after night during the imminent German offensive. On the high road between two big towns we passed the site of our future aerodrome.

The road lay over a succession of well wooded, seemingly interminable ravines with narrow gullies and defiles on each side. Our big car swung up and over the hills and down into the intervening

We Get a New Machine

valleys in the manner of a liner riding the long rollers of the Atlantic—evenly and with no sign of effort.

"Jolly bad country for forced landings, my boy," said my pilot. "Wouldn't care to 'conk' over here on a dark night!"

Presently we breasted a steeper incline than any we had hitherto met; the valleys lay behind us; ahead stretched a vast plateau across which, straight as a shot from a rifle, ran the new military road to the aircraft park. A mile down the road we saw the hangars and workshops of one of the largest aerial camps in France. In the air were machines of all kinds—Camels, Spads, Bristol Fighters, R.E. 8s, De Havillands, even dear old F.E.s. Some were arriving from England; some, having done their war service, had been flown from the squadrons and would later be sent back to England for use in training and home defence units; others were being tested prior to issue to the service squadrons in the line. It was a scene of aerial activity such as I have never witnessed before, and it produced on me an impression of steady organisation, vast resources, patience, courage, and imagination. For the first time I consciously realised the miracle of England's aerial effort.

We drove down to the office of the technical adjutant, presented our credentials, and were taken to the armament workshops, where we inspected our new weapon and were instructed in its use. The mounting and shell-racks, however, were not then quite complete, and we were informed that we should not be allowed to fly away that day.

After tea snow-clouds drifted up and the wind increased in violence. We stood out on the aerodrome and watched an R.E. 8 crash badly, though, fortunately, neither pilot nor observer was injured. Five minutes later the snow and hail came, blotting out the landscape.

"Tommy is not down yet. He took a Camel up just before tea," one of the sectional pilots informed us, as we waited in lee of one of the hangars. Then, above the whining of the wind and the lashing of the hail, we heard the steady hum of a machine. It passed, flying low over the hangars, turned down the wind, and was gone in a flash, swallowed up in that savage, swirling mist of hail.

"He can't do it. He can't land in *this*," said

We Get a New Machine

one of the younger pilots. "Why doesn't he climb away from it, run before the wind, and land somewhere in a clear patch where there isn't any storm?"

"Oh, you don't know Tommy," retorted one of the test men. "He'll get down all right: Tommy always makes his best landings in weather like this. He *loves* it."

But even the test man could scarcely conceal his anxiety when we heard that tornado of sound approaching us again and saw the Camel about fifty feet above the aerodrome, rocked and buffeted like a cork on an angry sea. Once more she turned on a steep bank into the wind. For a second she seemed to hang there poised in mid-air; then the wind caught her and she darted, swallow-like, into the snow veil. When next we saw her she was two hundred feet over the aerodrome coming down in a steep spiral.

The test man breathed again. "She's all right," he muttered, sucking at his unlit pipe; "under perfect control! He'll pull her out of the spiral and land like a feather."

And he did. He touched ground at ninety miles an hour, dead into the wind and with full engine; yet his machine stopped running within ten yards. I have seen many exhibitions of clever piloting, but Tommy's hurricane landing that winter afternoon in France has remained longest in my memory.

Bad weather detained us at the depot for three days. Then the issue section formally handed us our machine, together with the watches, compasses, and other instruments which belonged to it, and we flew northward to our aerodrome. The afternoon was fine though gusty. We did the hundred and twenty odd miles in eighty minutes, arriving over the aerodrome at four thousand feet in a patch of wonderful sunshine.

My pilot was in joyous mood, and so was I. Our engine was pulling strongly, throbbing through the crisp air, through wind and eddies, drifts and streams. We gloried in her. Never had we flown a more perfect engine or such a joy of a "bus."

My pilot "biffed" me on the head. "She's a topper, boy! Perfectly rigged. Sweetest engine you ever saw. Hold tight! I'm going to spin."

We did eight or nine perfect spins to the right, then eight or nine to the left, and pulled out at four

We Get a New Machine

hundred feet. They were " pukha " spins, and the sensation was one of absolute security and reliance.

We made a fast landing and taxied up to the Tarmac. The fellows crowded round to see our new gun, and for the rest of the evening " Little Bertha " was the chief topic of conversation.

CHAPTER XII

OUR FIRST GUN RAID

EARLY next morning we arranged to test the efficiency of our new gun. A mound composed of stones, tin cans, and refuse in a field near the aerodrome had been chosen as a target; we loaded the shell-racks with our little high explosive and incendiary beauties; then, after making sure that the field was clear and that no one could approach it while our experiments were being carried out, we climbed to a thousand feet before beginning our glide down to the target. At five hundred feet I trained the gun and fired the first shell. A second or two later it burst within a few yards of the mound, and we heard its detonation even above the noise of our engine. Climbing again, we reloaded, turned back into the wind, and once more trained our aerial cannon, hoping this time to get an O.K. shot on to the mound. During this second glide down I managed to fire three shells, one high explosive and two incendiaries. The

Our First Gun Raid

former sent up a black column of earth a yard to the left of the base of the mound; one of the incendiaries was seen burning fiercely among the heap of tin cans; the remaining shell exploded several yards short. We flew round the field again and got off several more rounds, including two direct hits; then, satisfied with the results of our tests, we came down.

Captain M——, my pilot, was hugely delighted.

"That is the medicine to administer unto them," he shouted, as we taxied up to the hangars.

The C.O. also was pleased.

"You'll have the Huns guessing to-night," he said. "Those H.E. shells seem particularly savage. They come whining through the air, and burst sharply like 'whiz-bangs.'"

There was, therefore, a good deal of excited conjecture as to what the result of our adventure would be when, at eleven o'clock that night, the "Squadron Gun" left the aerodrome on its first experimental raid.

We were given a roving commission—that is, we had permission to attack any legitimate targets which presented themselves: trains, transports, or troops on the road, searchlights, dumps, aerodromes, batteries in action, or anti-aircraft defences. The moon was nearly at the full, visibility was perfect, and the night was still and cloudless. We climbed rapidly towards the lines, our plan of campaign being to cross over at a fairly considerable height with our engine well throttled back. We wanted plenty of height to play about in while we were looking for a target.

My pilot and I always managed to work in very close co-operation. If I spotted anything unusual, my method was to point it out to him, and we then decided as to the advisability of getting nearer to it, or farther away, as the case might be. If, on the other hand, he saw something first, he attracted my attention either by hitting me on the head or wobbling the joy-stick so that the " bus " swung from side to side.

"What do you make of that?" he would say. "Shall we go down and have a look at it?"

All I could see, perhaps, was a black blob on a road, or a cloud of steam. "How's the engine running?" I asked him, because a great deal depends on your distance from the line and the sweetness of your engine.

"Thumbs up!" he bawled.

Our First Gun Raid

" Right-ho ! " I replied. " Down we go ! "

That is how we worked it on this night of our first gun raid.

Although we were flying with a " roving commission," we had decided between ourselves to pay a visit to our old friends on the big Gotha aerodrome near Rumbeke. One night a few weeks earlier Captain M—— had been presented with a record " packet of hate " by the defences of this aerodrome. He had been nearly shot down, and had only managed to get back to our side of the lines by the skin of his teeth.

He was, therefore, particularly glad of the opportunity, which the arrival of our " Little Bertha " gave him, for the execution of a long overdue retaliation. And *some* retaliation it proved to be!

We flew over " Wipers " at five thousand feet. The guns were silent. We looked down over a desolate world bathed in soft moonlight, a world scarred and pocked like the face of a dead old man.

Zonnebeke Lake and the canals and moats of these ancient Flemish lowlands caught the moonshine, caressing it tenderly. There were no lights in the trenches, no sign that down there a million men waited to deal and to accept death. It was one of those silent periods when the puissant monster of war crouches and waits.

Meanwhile the forward companies guard and patrol ceaselessly. Presently the battle will be reformed; violence and pain will begin again.

Over Roulers we got a few bursts of "archie." The big wood for which we were making lay ahead. A village, which we knew to be crowded with German billets, stretched along its eastern edge; the Gotha aerodrome bordered its southern side, with the big hangars camouflaged by the trees.

We kept clear of the wood, flying well to the south of it, then swung our machine round, throttled down to about a thousand "revs.," and headed straight for the village. An observer in another machine a mile or so on our starboard side was firing his Lewis gun into the village. I could see the trail of sparks from the exhaust and the red stream of his tracer-bullets. Several searchlights had come on and were swinging round in wide arcs, searching for the raiding machines; some machine-guns were firing from the corner of the wood; and suddenly I heard the bark of anti-aircraft guns. I

Our First Gun Raid

began to think it was time to spring our surprise on the Huns.

The village was now less than a mile ahead, its ruined buildings agleam in the moonshine. I signalled my pilot to begin our glide, trained my gun and fired. There was a blinding flash from the muzzle of the gun and what appeared to be a sheet of flame nearly a foot long. This we had not noticed when testing " Little Bertha " in the daytime, although we afterwards discovered that it was quite a normal phenomenon. The flame, however, was more apparent than real; on dark nights it would seem to be more intense than on moonlight nights; in the daytime one scarcely noticed it.

Our blood was up, and we " strafed " those billets to the tune of well over twenty shells. After I had fired the first two or three of them all the anti-aircraft defences in the neighbourhood gave up the ghost. Searchlights, " onion " batteries, machine-guns, even dear old " archie "—all were obviously puzzled by these new missiles that were hurtling down upon them from the night sky. Never before had we been over a well-defended area with so little opposition. We could not claim, of course, to have actually *hit* any battery or gun or searchlight. We may have done so, but at night it is impossible to judge with absolute accuracy the location of targets of this type, so carefully are they camouflaged and concealed. But whether our shells executed any *material* damage in the village or not, it is certain that they had a *moral* effect, the importance of which may be judged by the complete paralysis of the defence organisation of the village. This effect we often noted subsequently, and other machines on which the new gun was later mounted reported similar experiences to ours.

After firing between twenty and thirty shells we flew over the wood and attacked the Gothadrome from a height of about fifteen hundred feet. For several minutes we seemed to have matters all our own way; then some gunners in the heart of the wood put a couple of shells too near us to be pleasant. I saw the twin flashes of their guns, and almost at the same moment heard the shells burst slightly above us. My pilot wobbled his joy-stick to some effect; I stood up in my seat and leaned over. He had opened his engine full out, but above its clamour I heard him shout :

Our First Gun Raid

"I'm going to dive on that battery in the wood. Try to get a couple of high explosives near it. After that sit down and keep your head in the 'office,' because I'll want to climb."

A few seconds later we dived steeply with full engine. I had to guess the position of the battery, which at that moment was inactive. I remember wondering whether their gunners were still standing by or had disappeared into some dug-out. Then I fired, reloaded and fired again. The shells burst savagely, and I hoped their bite was as vicious as their bark.

After that little parting demonstration we "zoomed" and climbed away for home and bed.

CHAPTER XIII

WE "STRAFE" A TRAIN

OUR second raid with "Little Bertha" was a most exciting affair. We were under orders to bomb some big sidings several miles over the lines, then on our return journey to keep a keen look-out for trains. We crossed the trenches without arousing any "hate," reached our objective and dropped our "pills" from about two thousand feet. Then, leaving the sidings behind us, we climbed to about five thousand feet and commenced to cruise round in wide circles, keeping an average distance of from ten to fifteen miles behind the lines.

Suddenly I saw a trailing cloud of steam on the loop line from T——, and thence to one of the most important German railheads. I jumped up, leaned over the pilot's wind-screen and shouted:

"A train, old boy—down there on the line from T——."

We held the usual rapid consultation. When you

We "Strafe" a Train

want to speak to your pilot in a "pusher" machine you can use your telephone if you like, but it seems more friendly and companionable to bend over and talk to him. He throttles down his engine, and if you get your heads below the "stream-line" of the machine you can hear each other without effort.

But you can't see his eyes through his goggles. He seems to you a figure of mystery—an automaton of the air. On the ground he is a fellow in his twenties—just as you are, interested in sport, girls, the newest show in town, the latest issue of *La Vie Parisienne*. But in the air he is the king of sportsmen, the master of the most daring of man's inventions. He challenges space, wind, storm, darkness, and wins—or loses—gaily.

Having made up our minds that the snaky-looking cloud of steam was in reality a troop or ammunition train, we dived for it, dived steeply through four thousand feet of space, a great black hawk of the night, swooping down to destroy.

At a thousand feet I opened fire, and saw a burst on the metals just in front of the locomotive. By this time half the train was in a loop section, the forward half was on the main line. We flew alongside the train at five hundred feet. My third or fourth shot caused a curious little blue flame in the locomotive itself, and the train came to a standstill. We again dived until we were just a few feet over the telegraph poles, pumping stuff into the carriages and wagons as hard as I could make my new weapon work.

"Little Bertha" spoke to some effect that night!

For five minutes we flew up and down that train. In the clear moonshine I could see little dark figures running from the danger zone into the fields on each side of the railway, running this way and that, seeking shelter and mercy from the flying death. Then a cool-minded and courageous little group of soldiers got a machine-gun out of the remains of the train, set it up in a meadow near the derelict locomotive, and started firing at us.

They must have been brave men, for, quite apart from anything else, the spectacle of a big night-bombing machine diving and "zooming" and turning so near the ground is enough to test the stoutest nerves. However, these grey-coated fellows got their gun along, and for two or three minutes spiritedly returned our fire and gave us a very hot time.

At one point, so near were their shots that we had to fly down the railway for a mile or so. The air "zipped" with bullets. We returned, however, for a final inspection of the train. Flying over it at between two and three hundred feet, we saw that two of the coaches were smouldering and that some of our shells had evidently damaged the permanent way, for the locomotive had left the metals and seemed to be lying on its side.

I fired a few more rounds into the ruins and at the spot where I imagined the machine-gun to be, then, in order to reduce head-resistance, crouched down in my "office" with my head below the "stream-line" of the machine.

An hour later we landed safely at our aerodrome.

CHAPTER XIV

SENTINEL SEARCHLIGHTS

FLYING in a "pusher" machine at night-time gives one a feeling of isolation which no other experience on earth can provide. You hear the steady reverberations of your engine, throbbing, thrumming, thundering behind you. You lean out of your "office" to compare the landmarks over which you are flying with your map, and the air sings swiftly past your ear-flaps. Beneath, around, and above you is one vast void of darkness.

In night flying anything from eight to ten thousand feet is considered a "safe" height. At this altitude we could afford to have a little sport with the Hun searchlights, and I imagine that tiger-hunting is tame compared with searchlight-dodging at some of the "hot spots" on the Western Front.

Of course, there are searchlights *and* searchlights. It all depends on the men behind them.

Sentinel Searchlights

Most night-flying pilots in time got to know which were the dangerous and which were the merely " funny " searchlights. I remember once when Bobby, one of our most experienced pilots, came back from a raid and said, " Those fellows at X got on to my tail to-night, and it took me all my time to shake them off."

" Those fellows at X," " The Twins at C," " The group along the edge of the forest at Z "— all these were searchlights admired but not courted. On the other hand, there were operators so naive and bluffable that it was a sheer delight to play with them. This you did by " camouflaging " your engine. You opened it full out for twenty seconds or so. Immediately anything from two to a dozen sinister fingers of light prodded and probed the sky in your direction. If it was a " hot spot " you got ready to dodge; if you knew they were " mugs " you grinned and signalled " thumbs up " to your observer.

But it cannot be denied there *were* unhealthy localities so far as searchlights are concerned, groups of lights controlled by exceptionally clever men. And it always afforded us great satisfaction if, by some new " stunt " or combination of "stunts," we could avoid being "picked up" and held in their beams.

I have seen German machines searched for, caught, held and shot down. One night over Amiens I saw a couple of big German bombers held in the beams of at least a dozen converging lights for fully five minutes. Vainly they "side-slipped," dived and "zoomed"; always those active, menacing, radiant bars of light followed and imprisoned them. One of these night raiders came down in flames; the other got away, but we have reason to believe that it was badly damaged.

On the night with which this sketch deals we left the ground-flares in great style, flew twice round the aerodrome, gaining height, then commenced to climb steadily for the lines. After ten minutes' flying due east we glimpsed away and ahead of us that palpitating line of flame which was the frontier of the war.

Just before we crossed the lines a big fire—probably a shell-dump—blazed up fiercely, then died away. This and the violent artillery "strafe" enabled us to get over the battle zone without being heard; the noise of our engine was drowned in the greater voice of the guns.

Sentinel Searchlights

We arrived in the neighbourhood of Bapaume at about six thousand feet. Suddenly, five miles or more away, several searchlights opened up, stabbing the sky in our direction above, below, and at the level at which we were flying. Yet not one of them managed to pick us up. We dodged them all with ease. They were all of the "funny" variety. We "throttled down," the operators lost us, and we watched the long, sinister tentacles of light erratically probing the sky for us—moving here and there, sometimes slowly searching a cloud, at other times frantically sweeping in great arcs from east to west, from north to south, and back again.

Then we opened our engine up again. The searchlights swung here and there aimlessly, without direction. My pilot signalled "danger over," and we flew on.

An hour later, in a more distant part of Hunland, quite near an aerodrome then being used by Richthofen's circus, two crossed searchlights, without any warning at all, suddenly got on to us and held us in a steady embrace. Immediately their barrage opened. There were bursts and spurts of fire in the air all round us; streams of vicious little red "tracer" bullets whizzed past us; strings of "flaming onions" curled up towards us. We banked and side-slipped, dived, "zoomed," and stalled, but all to no effect.

I have often wondered since whether or no von Richthofen was watching these aerial acrobatics.

It was apparent that the operator in charge of these twin searchlights had laid a trap for us, waiting until we were practically over his position before opening out. He was obviously not of the "funny" variety, this sentinel of the night. When we had succeeded in getting away from his lights he handed us on to two others.

This was cleverly and deliberately done.

The two other searchlights blazed up, swung slowly towards us, and adjusted themselves to the angle of the original two; the first pair then shut down. All this time we were being "hated" violently. Eventually the second pair of searchlights handed us on to a third pair. We went through the hottest ten minutes of all our flying experiences. Yes, there are searchlights *and* searchlights!

We finally got out of the beams and found our-

Sentinel Searchlights

selves once more in the friendly darkness. But we had been badly handled. On our return we discovered that our planes had been shot through in nearly twenty places. Our consolation was that, notwithstanding the clever manipulation of their searchlights and the violence of their barrage, we had succeeded in dropping our bombs on Richthofen's aerodrome.

CHAPTER XV

MY LONGEST FLIGHT

ONE of my earliest and most exciting "shows" proved eventually to be also my longest flight in the air, either by day or night. It was in the depth of winter, when the nights are long and flying risks—due to low clouds, local ground mists, and sudden squalls—are at their maximum.

We "took the air" about eleven o'clock with orders to fly up to the line and see what the weather looked like. If it promised to be at all treacherous we were to return. The target was a large aircraft-receiving depot which had never been attacked before. The distance to it was so considerable that to accomplish it we required the most favourable weather conditions.

We left the aerodrome that night fully expecting to be driven back by a snowstorm which had been threatening all the afternoon and evening, and which our most experienced weather

My Longest Flight

prophets predicted would arrive in our area about midnight.

I remember that as I walked out to my machine I caught a glimpse of the C.O. staring anxiously eastwards. It was apparent that he was reluctant to send us off on a hazardous "show" with the elements so much against us; but the strafing of this aircraft park was considered to be of vital importance.

All pilots and observers had also been asked to bring back certain information for the Aerial Intelligence Department. In my rough note-book under this date I find the entries: "Are there two lights or only one at X?" "Is there a particularly strong lighthouse at Y? If so, what does it flash?" "Try to give the exact location of the red flares N.W. of Z." And I remember studying these questions by the light of my hand-torch as we flew towards the line.

Beneath, around and above us was one vast void of blackness; we could just see the dull reflection of our navigation lights, which in bad weather we generally kept switched on until we were nearing the lines. I had to strain below and ahead for such lights and landmarks as I could pick up—a railway station, a bend in the river with some stray glint of starshine upon it, a peculiarly shaped blob of woodland, a land lighthouse flashing its recognition signal—always a friendly beacon to those who fly by night. Another machine, bent on some similar mission to our own, loomed on our port bow, her lights gleaming.

For a space she kept company with us, blinking her signal lamps in token of friendliness, then she veered off, and we lost her in the abounding vastness of the sky.

A mile or so across the lines that night we flew into some of the thickest clouds I have seen in the whole of my flying experience—layer upon layer of dense, brutal stuff.

We climbed to six thousand feet before we reached the "ceiling" of the mist, then quite suddenly we found ourselves floating under a clear sky. Ahead of us loomed further banks of cloud, looking for all the world like gently undulating foothills. Behind them, again, were great mountains of mist, holding the horizon, turrets and pinnacles, weird, fantastic needles standing out like white enamel against the intense black of the sky.

My Longest Flight

We were flying now solely by compass. As we came towards these cloud-mountains their outlines faded away imperceptibly; the snow patches and towering peaks seemed to melt together into a white haze, and for another thirty minutes we flew through a dense fog.

We were just beginning to consider the advisability of swinging the "bus" round and returning home when we heard a couple of ominous "woufs" in the neighbourhood of our tail.

"Archie," I muttered to myself.

"How the blazes have they picked us up in this stuff?" Two seconds later we ran out of the clouds into a perfectly clear patch, and the Hun started to "hate" us vigorously.

My pilot "stunted" as he had rarely stunted before, side-slipping, stalling, spiralling steeply, banking vertically. A couple of searchlights picked up our tail and hung on to us obstinately. It took us nearly five minutes to shake them off, and even after that we saw them probing and stabbing the upper heavens in a frantic effort to pick us up again.

For the first time since we crossed the lines

I was able to see the ground and to identify features on it.

We were over a large town which, by its shape, I knew to be Y——, a vital centre of railway and road communications. Our target lay some ten miles or so beyond.

We were able now to fly with the aid of our map and ground features. A few minutes later we saw the aerodrome, and dropped some of our " pills " on the hangars and the remainder on some railway sidings near by. Curiously enough, we met here with no resistance at all.

The target had not been attacked before, and it was obvious that for once we had caught the Hun napping.

" Little Bertha " had been left alone that night, and I had on board my old Lewis gun. We circled over the aircraft park for two or three minutes, and although visibility was poor, and I could not observe clearly the results of either bombing or firing, I got off over a hundred rounds before my gun jammed. We put our nose west once more, flying almost immediately into fog and rain.

Occasionally we caught a fleeting glimpse of

My Longest Flight

the newly risen moon through scudding wracks of storm cloud. The temperature had gone down and the wind had both increased in velocity and changed in direction.

For a short time we flew through blinding snow.

During the snowstorm our compasses started to swing. We went on blindly, hoping to get out of the clouds and pick up some landmark.

After between two and three hours of this we caught a glimpse of what appeared to be moonshine on the sea.

"We've got to land!" my pilot shouted. "Petrol running low! Fire off a few Verey lights; perhaps one of the coast aerodromes will light up for us."

I did this, but nothing happened.

"Right-ho!" he said cheerfully. "Unscrew the gun. Try and pick out a field."

I glued my eyes earthwards through the mist. We were rapidly losing height. Presently I saw the lights of a town, and we flew towards them. Red and green signal lamps, steam from a locomotive showed us that we were over a railway station. We flew round once or twice at about a hundred feet, then my pilot " chanced it " and put the " bus " down perfectly in a small field alongside the railway.

Not a wire had been strained; it was one of the best forced landings I have ever had by day or night.

Even then, so blind had we been during the latter part of our flight, we were not sure whether we were down in Hunland or on our side of the lines. A great crowd of railway workers swarmed across the field to us. With a good deal of relief I heard English voices. That was about four o'clock in the morning. We found we had drifted down south and were only about an hour's flying from our own aerodrome.

At six o'clock that morning, just as dawn was breaking, we requisitioned petrol and hot water from the railway people, filled our tanks, started our " prop," flew the " bus " out of the field, and arrived home in time for breakfast, having been in the air nearly six hours.

CHAPTER XVI

THE TECHNICAL STAFF

THE Map-Room is the centre of the business life of every squadron on active service. In it you receive all orders for operations, study your course, work out your compass-bearings, "pin-point" your objectives. You often think of it when you are in the air; sometimes it flits disturbingly through your dreams at night.

You do not go to the Map-Room for quiet meditation. It is not a chapel of ease. It is the board-room, the inner sanctum of your flying life. It is terribly businesslike. Its walls bristle with *facts*. When you are in the air you realise the poetry of flying. *Sometimes!* The Map-Room is its *prose*. You go there to stare at the large and small scale maps which adorn its walls; to read the latest reports from Branch and Wing Intelligence; to study the photographs of aerodromes and towns, trench systems and battery positions; to admire the terse communiqués from the Armies and from Air Force Headquarters; finally, to read your own squadron orders, wing orders, brigade orders and G.R.O.s.

The Map-Room is the apotheosis of work.

In a night-flying squadron you make your way to the Operation-Room about five o'clock every afternoon. "Operation-Room" is only a more official way of describing the Map-Room. When all pilots and observers have been reported present the C.O. comes in, officially announces the target, and reads out the operation orders for the night. Most C.O.s have themselves been through the "soup." They know what it is to "sit on" "archie," to hear the pop-pop of tracer bullets round your head, or the ominous "woufs" of shells bursting in the neighbourhood of your tail. They, too, have seen those long, sinister fingers of light which prod and probe the night sky in quest of your machine, and the strings of "flaming onions" which are flung upwards at you in coils and spirals, sprays and corkscrews. Most C.O.s, therefore, say a few quiet words in the Map-Room before you start on your "show."

"Cheerio, you fellows! Give the searchlights at M—— a wide berth. The operator there is

The Technical Staff

rather a nut, and if he once gets on to you you'll find him a difficult customer to deal with."

Then when you have donned your flying kit you go out to your machine. The C.O. stands on the aerodrome and watches his big bombers "taxi" out to the flare-path and throb eastwards into the night. On your return he is waiting for you, either in his office or in the Operation-Room, and he listens to the tale of your journey, often asking you to point out on the map places where you had observed things of interest to the powers that be.

Next in importance to the Map-Room is the Gun-Room, the headquarters of the squadron Armament Officer. In this holy of holies all the guns of the squadron are stored, cleaned, and repaired; gears and gadgets are tested; records of jams and stoppages are filed; and ammunition is cleaned, loaded into drums or belts, and issued to the warriors who will later use it against the enemy. The Armament Officer is a figure of importance in squadron life, especially in those squadrons where guns are used which fire through the propeller, as then he has not only to thoroughly understand the mechanism of his various types of guns, but he must also be an expert on synchronising gears.

It is not generally known that every gun in the air service—like every machine and every engine—has its "log-book," in which is recorded in minute detail its official history, the number of rounds it has fired, the number and nature of each stoppage or jam, the dates of renewal of parts, and the spring pressure and other conditions under which it gives its best results. A good armament officer knows from the history of his guns when to retire them from active service and pension them off. A "dud" gun is worse than no gun, because a man cannot afford to go into an aerial fight with a weapon which he imagines may fail him at the critical moment. It tends to make him "windy" and to deteriorate his moral.

The ultimate success of war in the air depends entirely on three factors—the maintenance of moral and sufficiency and efficiency of material. To this end the Gunnery Officer is fulfilling a rôle which in the future will, if anything, increase in importance.

Side by side with the gunnery man is the

The Technical Staff

Equipment Officer, who is responsible for all the kit, stores, tents, huts, lorries, cars, tenders, oil, petrol, fuel or furniture issued or loaned to the squadron. In the airman's hegemony he looms as a person of vast importance possessing certain arbitrary powers. He is a useful man to know. When you are coming home on leave, for instance, he can *sometimes* "wangle" a tender for you all the way down to Boulogne. When you want a joy-ride into Amiens or St. Pol or St. Omer you can watch his movements carefully, then nip in at the right moment and, stroking your hair, mention the fact that you know an excellent barber in the Rue Voltaire or the Petit-Place.

The Equipment Officer can also occasionally be an avenging demon of wrath. These moods overcome him periodically, disturbing his digestion and his temper, and they arise in connection with such mundane things as "crash watches," missing map-cases or goggles, hand-torches, batteries, electric light bulbs, and fur collars—"officers, for the use of." These and other troubles—mainly in connection with demand for transport—drive most equipment officers to the verge of suicide

98   Rovers of the Night Sky

until suddenly they receive their promotions to wing jobs. Then they smile once more, abuse the "no-treating" order, and someone else reigns in their stead.

The Photographic and Wireless Officers complete the technical staff of the squadron. Night-flying squadrons only see photographic officers on rare occasions. Generally speaking, "picture-taking" is a function of "corps" machines and long-distance day-flyers. Pictures of trench systems, enemy batteries, dumps, and field fortifications are taken by machines working along each corps frontage; photographs of new roads, railways, sidings, hutments, camps and aerodromes behind the immediate battle area are obtained by long-distance reconnaissance machines. These photographs, however, are often of great value to night-flyers, especially those which show the country behind the trench zone. In certain conditions of moonlight the landscape beneath you very closely resembles a photograph. It is indeed a moot point as to whether or no a series of specially prepared photographic maps would not be of more use for night navigation than are the ordinary ordnance survey maps in general use. For this

The Technical Staff

reason a closer alliance is needed between photographic officers and night-flying units.

The Wireless Officer, like the Gunnery Officer, is a man whose job is increasing in importance with every advance in aerial science. At present his work consists mainly in fitting up machines with wireless sets, in testing and repairing those sets, and in taking reports whenever a wireless " bus " is in the air. It is not an exciting job, but it provides interesting moments, as when a certain enthusiast, ordered to test the weather, decided that it was too " dud " for the squadron to do a " show," but that it was good enough for him personally to do one. He left the aerodrome and disappeared eastward. We all expected him to come down and land within a quarter of an hour. But time passed and nothing was seen or heard of our hero. Then a jubilant message flashed back across a stormy sky.

" Rivers and roads invisible at three thousand. Can only see gun-flashes. Am going to cross the line. Perhaps it is better on the other side."

A few minutes later a further message arrived.

" Am somewhere near Bapaume."

"Much 'hate'—'archie' and machine-guns. Clouds at fifteen hundred."

We crowded into the wireless office for further bulletins. The next report came through after an anxious quarter of an hour.

"Raining! Dropped bombs on Bapaume. Engine knocking badly. Am returning."

Then for nearly an hour the night was a void of silence. Several times we went out on to the aerodrome, but there were no lights or signals, no welcome drone of engine in the sky, only low-scurrying clouds and gusts of wind and rain.

Finally came a frantic appeal.

"Am lost. Please fire rockets."

We fired the rockets and made quite a pyrotechnic display with Verey lights and flares and what not. And we rang up neighbouring aerodromes to let them know we had a machine up, and "would they put their ground-flares out and also fire rockets at intervals." All this because we wanted our foolish bird to "home." He had done a brave thing to fly through this stormy night sky, and although we were angry at his foolhardiness we admired his pluck.

A few minutes after midnight we saw his lights

The Technical Staff

blinking low over the trees. His engine was evidently at its last gasp, but he was nursing it home. He came round on a dangerous bank over the hangars and put her down into the flare-path, bumping badly and landing on the third bump. But he was down. That was all that mattered to us. We drifted in twos and threes into the mess to have a drink and forget about war and aeroplanes and rash young pilots who "chance" Bapaume on a "dud" night. We didn't even wait to congratulate the bird on "homing." That came later when we first gave him a drink, and then used him as one uses a rugger ball in a scrimmage.

CHAPTER XVII

HINTS

THE military importance of night-flying operations is now generally recognised; and the great increase in aerial activity at night is tending inevitably towards specialisation in the training of pilots and observers for night work. In a night-flying machine—whether its object be bombing, reconnaissance, or the machine-gunning of troops and transport on the road—the functions of the observer are equally as important as those of the pilot; and to this end the training of a night-flying observer has to be equally as thorough and scientific as that of a night-flying pilot.

Night-flying on a large scale is a comparatively new phase of war activity. During the last months of the war, however, it made remarkable progress, and events, if anything, served to emphasise its military importance. The chief objects of night-flying are the bombing of towns and other targets of military value behind the

Hints

enemy lines; the machine-gunning of ground objectives such as transport, troops, trains, and searchlights; the reconnoitring of roads, railways, aerodromes, and dumps; and aerial fighting.

The principal targets attacked were aerodromes; railway stations, junctions, and sidings; trains; roads with troops and transport on them; dumps of stores and ammunition; factories; hutments and camps; locks, docks, and bridges, guns and gun emplacements; and villages near the line where enemy troops were known to be billeted.

An observer's duties both on the ground and in the air are many. He is responsible for the condition of all the apparatus he will use during operations—guns, maps, lights, bomb-racks, bomb-releases, bomb-sights, and compasses. During night operations he is responsible for finding the way to and from the target, for aligning the machine on to the target and keeping the pilot directed by means of prearranged signals, for controlling the release of the bombs, and for firing the guns which all night-bombing machines carry.

It must be borne in mind that the pilot *flies* the machine, the observer *navigates* it. The reason for this is that an observer has more time at his disposal, in most machines has a wider view, and has more accommodation in his seat for maps. If, therefore, a machine is lost owing to faulty or careless navigation the onus of blame rests more upon the observer than upon the pilot, who, it is obvious, cannot be expected to look after his engine, fly his machine, and at the same time do the observer's work of watching the ground over which the machine is passing.

Good observation is becoming more and more essential in night-flying, and the value of a careful, conscientious observer cannot be overestimated. He must be able not only to find his way to and from his various objectives, but when he has found them he must be able to drop his bombs accurately upon them. He is required also to pay careful attention to reconnaissance work, noting any lights he may see, any aerodrome activity, all movements of trains, troops, and transport. He must be thoroughly familiar with his maps and be able accurately to " pin-point " localities. Finally, he should keep a constant look out for hostile aircraft.

To perform all these functions reliably he has

Hints

to work on the assumption that his pilot sees nothing and does nothing except fly the machine. What the pilot does see will help to substantiate or to correct his own observations. But no observer on landing after operations expects his pilot to make any other report than the customary one regarding the condition of his engine and the rigging or controls of his machine.

A good observer—whether he is a day or night flyer—should be able not only to fire his gun, he should be able to fire it with the maximum effect. He should be an expert on it.

A thorough understanding of maps and a rapid facility in reading them are of vital importance in night-flying.

When an observer first arrives at a squadron overseas he should obtain information as to the areas over which the squadron usually works. He should then set to work to *improve* his maps from a practical night-flying point of view, remembering that when he uses a map in a machine it will be dark; that it is necessary to be able to note any feature on it *at a glance;* and that as little artificial light as possible must be used, and for as short a time as possible.

He should mark in the "Line," distinctly noting any important places or landmarks on or near it, and any pronounced salients. He should next memorise the principal ground features and landmarks which he knows from experience or study will be useful to him while flying by night. He should note the order in which the landmarks will appear when flying from the aerodrome to various sectors of the line, and the relationship of the landmarks to each other. Aerial photographs will be found an invaluable aid in this respect, and as many as possible should be obtained, studied, and compared with the corresponding sections of the map.

Roads, railways and canals passing through towns; main roads and railways leading from one town to another; peculiarly shaped woods or lakes, railway junctions and cross-roads—all these should be carefully noted and visualised.

The railways should then be broadly inked over, so that they stand out prominently, a distinction being made between single and double tracked systems. The main roads should be made a deeper brown or red; the rivers, canals and lakes a deeper blue, and the woods a deeper green, the principle being that the more a landmark shows up at night from the air the more prominent it needs to be shown on the map.

The characteristics of different parts of the country and of rivers, locks, harbours and towns should be carefully memorised.

The country may be wooded or clear. If it is wooded the woods may be either grouped or isolated, large or small, or of some definite characteristic shapes; or the country may be open, close or swampy.

On many occasions even experienced airmen have mistaken swamps for rivers or for the sea—especially when mist has been hanging over them —owing to restricted range of vision at night.

A comparison between the rivers Lys and Escaut in Flanders illustrates the practical value of the study of river characteristics. Both rivers are canalised.

The Lys canal, however, follows the large natural bends and sweeps of the river, while the canalised Escaut, owing to the great number of small unnavigable bends in the river, has had to be cut straight across intervening country, with the result that all along its course there are small river loops enclosing small islets. Hence, although the rivers are not far apart, the Lys cannot possibly be taken for the Escaut even by night.

A study of the harbours at Zeebrugge, Blankenberghe, Ostend, Dunkirk, Calais, Boulogne and Havre, and of the docks at Bruges and Ghent, will testify to the fact that each harbour or dock has its own peculiar characteristics.

Fairly large towns appear by night as black masses with more or less distinctive outlines, and a study and comparison of their characteristic shapes and their positions with regard to rivers, railways and canals will yield interesting results.

Rough sketch maps should frequently be made of the main roads, rivers, railways, canals and woods in the area to be flown over.

Important cross-roads and railway junctions, and peculiar bends or turns in roads, railways or rivers should also be impressed upon the memory by means of rough sketches.

These map studies should be continued until the observer can recognise and interpret a sketch map of any part of his flying area, and can reproduce from memory a rough map of any part of the same area, with approximate accuracy.

Hints

If an observer will carry an ordinary rectangular protractor about with him, and use it on maps whenever he has a few spare moments, he will realise that distances and bearings need present no difficulty.

It cannot be too emphatically stated, however, that marks, figures, notes, lines or dots which have reference to features on our side of the line should not be inserted on any maps which are to be taken on a raid.

Lights or lighthouses in enemy territory may, however, be shown, as they often prove very useful. Information regarding such lights can be obtained from the Intelligence Sheets which are issued daily to squadrons.

Any new enemy military constructions, such as broad or narrow gauge railways, aerodromes, hutments and dumps, should also be inserted and kept up to date. Enemy Organisation Maps, which are issued periodically, show any fresh evidence of military activity.

CHAPTER XVIII

"BOBBY" IS MISSING

ABOUT the middle of January, 19—, our long-expected electrical clothing arrived, and after lunch one cold, dry, windy afternoon we decided to mount to the "ceiling" of our machine and see what sort of comfort our electrical socks and gloves and waistcoats would give us. The necessary batteries, plugs and generators had been installed during the morning, and about two o'clock we left the aerodrome, climbing in wide circles until hangars, and machines on the ground, and roads, packed with lorries, cars and men, appeared merely as fragments of a Lilliputian landscape.

The clouds floated beneath us, veiling the earth shyly; and still we climbed. Our engine was running powerfully, and we breasted ten thousand feet in a little over twenty minutes. It is wonderful to think of a two-ton weight pulling itself up through space and by its own power maintaining itself there.

"Bobby" is Missing

We climbed through the thinner layers of air, our engine thrumming steadily.

It was bitterly cold. Eastward, snowbanks were blowing over with the on-coming night; westward, the sun declined behind thick clouds. Below us a patrol of scouts raced homeward before the wind. I got the signal from my pilot to switch on our warming batteries. In a couple of minutes or less we felt their glow; in ten minutes we became so hot that we had to switch off for a space in order to cool down. And that at fifteen thousand feet!

We were satisfied with our electrical clothing, spiralled down from fifteen thousand—slowly, so that our hearing would not be affected—and landed in time for tea.

Several days of bad flying weather followed. On the last night in January we were ordered up to "test the weather," remained in the air for half an hour, then came down and got the stunt "washed out." On the first of February we flew down to an aerodrome in the mining country behind Bethune, and on the following night bombed a hostile battery near Menin. Then for seventeen days we did no service flying. All the mining lowlands remained shrouded in a dense pall of mist.

We played cards, got up concerts, visited all the infantry messes in the neighbourhood, did a little day-flying between intervals of fog, and commandeered cars and tenders for St. Pol and Lillers and Bethune, according to our respective tastes and the addresses of our lady friends. In other words, we "slacked."

On the night of the seventeenth of February, although the weather was unfavourable, we were detailed to bomb the German night-flying aerodrome at S——. We started immediately after tea, crossed the lines at dusk, reached our objective more by good fortune than skill, bombed it and flew homeward with the feeling that all war is futile. A few minutes before we regained our lines, however, I chanced to look over the side of the nacelle, and noticed that one of the bombs had not been released.

"Oh, bust it!" I said to myself. "We don't want to take it home."

So I tugged and pulled at the refractory release-lever, and it worked. I saw the bomb fall from the rack and drop earthwards. Ten seconds

"Bobby" is Missing

later there was a terrific detonation, a column of sparks, and a rapid up-blazing of flame. My pilot swung the "bus" round, and we saw that the glare proceeded from a blazing mass near the junction of two trunk roads. We had chanced on one of the enemy's petrol dumps, and our lucky bomb had fired it.

On the two following evenings we started out on bombing raids, but had to return owing to incredibly thick local ground-mists which swathed the lowlands like a gigantic grave-cloth.

On the twenty-first of February I did a "Special Duty" patrol with Capt. P., of the Intelligence Service.

Information had been given to the effect that a German machine, flying low over a certain area, was signalling and dropping messages nightly to spies concealed in or near a large wood several miles behind the lines. The Hun was supposed to be using a captured British machine of the type we were then flying; our job was to camouflage ourselves as the Hun aerial spy and endeavour to locate the exact spot on the ground from which he was in the habit of receiving his signals.

It was a perfect night. The mists had cleared. The air seemed crowded with machines; we passed several of our fellows outward-bound for Bapaume and for the " Fives " station at Lille and the Hun aerodrome at Marquain. German bombers were busy over Bethune, over the Isberque steelworks near Aire, and farther north over St. Omer. We could see the bursting of their bombs, and the shrapnel barrages put up by the British and French gunners round the areas attacked. And, eastward over the front, trailing spirals and corkscrews of " onions " filled the sky; evidently some of our machines were having a hot time.

I am not allowed to describe our work that memorable night. It will be sufficient to relate that we were successful in camouflaging ourselves as the Hun, that the spies actually signalled to *us*—using the head-lamps of a powerful car for that purpose—and that, although we were unable to decipher their code, we succeeded in locating their headquarters. More than that I cannot say.

We put our nose down and came home at between ninety and a hundred miles an hour. Over the aerodrome I fired our priority signal, and they let us land at once. French liaison officers of the Intelligence Service were waiting for our report, and several arrests were effected within a few hours.

Four days later M. and I were detailed for a line patrol after Gothas. We climbed to eight thousand feet, took "Little Bertha" with us, remained up for nearly three hours, saw no enemy machines whatever, and came down thoroughly disappointed.

The mist had drifted back from the sea and hung about with only rare and brief intervals of clearness. During one of these intervals I was detailed to show a new pilot round the country. On the way home we nearly flew into the big slag heaps at Auchel.

We had been up to Hazebrouck, and then over Kemmel nearly as far as "Wipers"; had flown back through low clouds and arrived over the aerodrome in a storm of hail and sleet. The hangars lay in lee of the slag heaps. The driving swirl hid everything from view. Suddenly I glimpsed the great slag cones looming less than fifty yards ahead of us. My pilot saw them a fraction of a second later, banked steeply and "got away with it." We landed neatly; and I must confess that I was never so profoundly glad to step out of an aeroplane.

That same evening, in squally and dangerous weather, we carried out another line patrol. We flew up and down the front between Armentières and St. Quentin for nearly four hours. It proved to be an uneventful show except for one incident the significance of which I did not realise until several months later. About half-way between Armentières and La Bassée, and several miles over the lines, I saw a machine going down in wide, controlled spirals and with wing-tip flares burning.

On our return I reported the matter to the Recording Officer. That night Bobby failed to return from the raid. We waited until eight o'clock next morning, for Bobby was one of our most popular men. Then the Casualty Report went in, "Machine Number 3,333 has not returned. Pilot, So-and-so. Observer, Lieutenant X——."

Nobody believed that Bobby had "gone West," for, although the weather had been gusty and dangerous, visibility had been good. You

"Bobby" is Missing

could pick out the character of the ground from a thousand feet, and everybody said:

"Bobby has landed on the other side. Poor old Bobby! A prisoner! No more poker for the duration, unless they play it in Karlsruhe."

Bobby was very fond of poker.

His observer, after four months' hell in various German camps, managed to escape. I ran across him casually in London, took him to a place where we could get a good feed without ostentation, and gleaned from him the story of his adventures.

Bobby's engine had developed trouble half-way between Menin and Courtrai, but, believing that he could nurse it home, he had carried on until it cut out altogether. Only those who have been through it can adequately realise the feeling of dismay and helplessness which comes over you when you hear your engine spluttering out, coughing and groaning over its last few revolutions. You will try all the dodges you know, but nothing happens. Then comes the silence before the crash; you hear only the singing of the wind in your wires as you glide down.

Bobby brought off a splendid forced landing

that night in a field near Courtrai. He got down without straining a wire; but they were in German territory, and twenty miles or so from the line. For ten minutes no one came to them, and during this time they were frantically tinkering at the engine in the hope of being able to remedy the defect and fly away before they were discovered.

Then a German non-commissioned officer arrived, accompanied by a guard of several men; Bobby and his observer were arrested and thrown for the remainder of the night into Courtrai civil prison. On the following day they were taken back to German Intelligence Headquarters, where elaborate attempts to pump them were made. Bobby and his friend, however, were of stout stuff, and the Hun interrogators got no change out of them.

Then followed a weary journey through Northern Belgium to a prison camp in Germany. Near the frontier they attempted to jump the train, but without success, and, as a punishment, their coats and boots were confiscated. They travelled in a third-class carriage occupied also by German soldiers returning home on leave. They suffered

"Bobby" is Missing

from cold and hunger, but most of all from the gibes and insults of the Hun soldiers.

In the prison camp they received harsh treatment. The slightest offence against the stringent and arbitrary rules was followed by a period of punishment—mainly solitary confinement in cells. Food was scarce and poor. There was no tea, cocoa, sugar, butter or meat; the sole beverage was acorn coffee; tinned sardines were purchasable, but only at exorbitant prices. The monotonous diet consisted of vegetable soups—principally potatoes—and a sandy, gritty kind of bread which was unpalatable and impossible to digest.

After some months of this all pilots and observers in that particular camp were separated; Bobby was taken farther east, his observer came west. And on the way thither the latter managed to crawl through the lavatory window of the train, dash into the shelter of some woods at the side of the railway, and make good his escape.

Fired at on several occasions, trailed by dogs, sleeping by day, journeying by night, stealing what food he could from farmhouses, he managed, in *British Air Force uniform,* to cover the two hundred odd miles which lay between the place of his escape and the frontier. On one occasion he walked in broad daylight, without any attempt at camouflage, on to the platform of a large country-town station; on another occasion he hid in a ditch for two days without food the while a vigorous search for him was being prosecuted in the neighbourhood.

Finally, worn, unkempt, haggard, he got through the live wire which marked the Dutch-German frontier, and was sent on to England by the Consul-General.

CHAPTER XIX

LITTLE COMEDIES

FROM a night observer's point of view, finding one's way in mists or clouds is a most difficult and trying operation. Usually, even on the darkest night, one can see lights in towns, fires in camps or billets, puffs of steam from locomotives on the railways, the starshine on rivers or patches of water, the head-lamps of cars on the road. But in damp weather you peer out of your "office"; suddenly a cross-road or stretch of railway or patch of water looms up at you through the swirling fog wreaths. You dive for your map in the hope of identifying the piece of country immediately beneath you, but by the time you have found out where you are your cross-road or railway or water-patch has been swallowed up in the mist again.

In treacherous weather even the best pilot or observer is apt to lose his whereabouts. To be lost at night-time is no joke, yet, curiously enough, the fellows who lose themselves seem almost invariably to meet with " comic " adventures which more than compensate them for any danger or discomfort they may have passed through. In our squadron we had a pilot whose name went through the Casualty Report no fewer than four times. Each time, however, he turned up during the following day none the worse for his experiences. He landed in fields of all sizes and descriptions—once near Paris, another time on the coast, then at Rouen, and once in a turnip field miles from anywhere. He brought back tales of pretty schoolmistresses who had befriended him, of dinners in châteaux, drinks with brigadiers, rides with " brass hats " in Staff cars, until we all envied him and wished that such phenomenal luck could befall us.

The most amazing part of all these incidents, however, was that he rarely broke anything on his machine. He pulled off the most lucky series of forced landings that I have heard of. Only on one occasion did he crash badly, and then he happened to be within a mile or two of the largest aircraft depot in France. All he did was to leave his wounded " bird " in the field where it had fallen, betake himself to the aforesaid depot, collect a new machine, and fly it home to the aerodrome.

About this time—a period of dangerous fogs and ground-mists—one of our oldest and most experienced night-flyers got hopelessly lost, and landed, as he imagined, near the coast in the German lines between Nieuport and Ostend. He and his observer clambered out, held a hasty consultation, and set fire to their machine. It burned merrily.

"The Germans may take *us*, my boy," declared the pilot grimly, "but they won't take our 'bus.'"

Then they walked along the shore for about an hour—and came upon a little bathing resort, *near Havre.*

Tableau! Collapse of two heroic airmen! They sheltered for the night in one of the Havre hospitals. When they eventually arrived back at the squadron they were received boisterously, and it was unsafe for any of us to mention the words "Fire" or "Havre" in their hearing for days and weeks afterwards.

Who of us will ever forget the malicious glee with which we welcomed the famous exploit of

Captain B. and his observer? Both were careful, shrewd men, both had nerves of steel, stout hearts and original ideas for outwitting the Hun. Both set out one misty, difficult evening to bomb a big German dump about five or six miles behind the lines. That evening we could scarcely see from one end of the aerodrome to the other. There was no wind and a dank, heavy mist shrouded the ground. In ordinary circumstances we should have regarded this as a "dud flying night," and the whole squadron would have betaken itself in motor-cars and tenders and lorries to the nearest town for dinner and a merry evening. As it was, however, we felt that it was "up to us" to take the air and "chance it," for the March offensive had begun and our comrades on the ground were fighting grimly to stem the tide of the German advance.

Captain B. and his observer left the aerodrome shortly after dusk, and at midnight we gave them up for lost. Every other machine had arrived back safely by ten o'clock.

Early next morning their machine, empty and abandoned, was found by some Canadian pioneers in a field not six miles from the aerodrome.

Little Comedies

There was no trace of either Captain B. or his observer. The machine was intact, undamaged, and, so far as we could see, had been landed while still under control. The neighbourhood was searched, hospitals were visited, ponds and wells were dragged, but without result. The two airmen had either fallen out of their machine while still in flight, their corpses lying in some inaccessible spot, or they had been spirited away.

For three days we mourned them, and were just getting accustomed to their absence when, one afternoon about tea-time, they walked into the ante-room wet, unkempt, ravenous. Their story was that they had landed their "bus," and then, believing themselves in Hunland, had "cut and run for it." And for three days they had remained in hiding, sleeping by day in the heart of a big wood, sallying forth at night in search of food and to try to find out where they were. Eventually they saw British soldiers, and walked back to the aerodrome. When they arrived they were crestfallen, sore, angry with themselves. But we soon cheered them up, pointing out that they had made a valuable contribution to the sum total of the squadron's gaiety.

About this time a big German night-bomber was severely damaged by our anti-aircraft fire and forced to land several miles behind our lines. The occupants—two German officers and a gunner-mechanic—first attempted to set fire to their machine. Failing in this, however, they strolled up to the nearest farmhouse, banged at the door, proudly informed the aged farmer and his wife that they were " Prussian aviator officers," and solemnly *demanded* supper, beer and disguises with which to escape from " those swine-pigs of Englanders."

In the meantime from the aerodrome we had watched the descent of the machine. Two or three of us, who were not flying that night, were sent out in the squadron car to find it and to arrest, if alive, its occupants. We traced the machine down and arrived at the farmhouse only just in time to save the Germans from being roughly handled. We found them surrounded by a crowd of French farm-hands, women and urchins, brandishing pitchforks, brooms, rusty knives and pieces of wood—as odd an assortment of warriors and weapons as I have ever seen. The Germans were vociferating in deep, threatening gutturals,

Little Comedies

and the crowd, thoroughly roused and angered by their preposterous behaviour, would, I believe, have given them short shrift had we not arrived at the critical moment and prevented the incident from developing into a summary lynching. They surrendered with a bad grace and were brought back to the aerodrome.

A night or two later my pilot and I were the unwitting causes of considerable amusement in the squadron. It was during the dark period; we had had a week of "dud" weather, and the conditions were unsafe for anything except a very short show. As an experiment, however, it was decided to send a wireless machine on a direct compass-course to a town in the German forward area with instructions to send back weather reports every five miles or so up to the line. Ours was the machine selected for the job. We left the aerodrome, flew for a certain number of minutes on a given compass-bearing, dropped a parachute flare, and by its light saw the target a short distance ahead, released our bombs and came home again. On walking into the mess for a drink we were greeted with cries of "Rockets! Rockets!" After a good deal of chaffing we were told that the only weather report received by the wireless operator on the aerodrome had been a continual repetition of "Rockets! I am lost. Send up rockets! Rockets!" We were able in the end, however, to convince our deriders that *we* were not the culprits, as shortly after leaving the ground I had discovered that our aerial was broken. We had then decided to fly straight to our target without coming down for a new aerial, and because of this we had not been able to send a single message. On the following morning our version was verified. The frantic screams for " Rockets ! " had come from a new pilot in another squadron who had been sent up for a practice " flip " round the lighthouses.

Another of these little comedies nearly developed into a tragedy.

For a week or more a daring Hun, flying a captured British machine, had been crossing our lines regularly about five o'clock every afternoon and bombing Bethune. As a counter-stroke two machines from different squadrons were ordered to fly along the canal between La Bassée and Bethune with instructions to shoot down at sight any F.E. machine they came across. " Monty,"

Little Comedies

one of the crack merchants of X squadron, was one of the pilots chosen for this job. "Daisy," the giant of our own squadron, was the other.

Both pilots carried observers of the keen, fire-eater type.

They flew off from their respective aerodromes, but although they remained up for several hours they saw no marauding Hun; instead they met each other. Above Bethune under a lowering sky "Monty" and "Daisy" circled round seeking for an opportunity of spitting fire and death from their guns. Their circles became narrower; often their wing-tips passed within a few feet of each other; yet each failed continually to get up behind the other's "blind" spot.

Our man's observer at last managed to get his gun trained on the other squadron's pilot when suddenly he recognised in his doughty opponent none other than the celebrated "Monty."

"A fraction of a second later," he said, when recounting the incident, "I should have pulled my gun and 'Monty' would have been a dead man sure. Couldn't have missed! Fortunately 'Daisy' recognised him almost at the same moment, and we side-tracked out of the fight."

Little comedies like these made up the lighter side of an airman's life in France. They are touchstones to much gaiety and mirth. They served to take our thoughts away from the great strain and stress which are inevitable on active service.

CHAPTER XX

BEFORE THE OFFENSIVE

EARLY in March, 1918, we migrated still farther south to an aerodrome behind Arras. So far as surroundings and quarters were concerned, this was the best aerodrome we flew from during my service with the squadron. On the night following our arrival we did our first "show" from the new aerodrome. It was a pitch-black night aggravated by low clouds and high winds. As we neared the lines our engine started to miss badly. We decided, however, that we would just cross over, drop our bombs and trust to St. Michael to get us home again. We passed over the trenches at less than a thousand feet without attracting any unwelcome attentions. There was no gun-fire yet. Both sides seemed to be nervous. I had never before seen so many lights and rockets fired from the ground. I imagine that patrols were busy that night. It was just before the opening of the German drive on Amiens and Paris.

We dropped our bombs, so far as we could judge, on the reserve positions, fired a few shells from " Little Bertha," then put our nose down and made for home, carefully nursing our engine. We landed just in time. An examination of our engine showed that a small end of one of the cylinders had cracked; our flight-sergeant informed us that she could not possibly have lasted more than another five minutes or so.

On the following morning a wire came through from the Wing that my pilot had been awarded the Military Cross. We celebrated the event with a "fizz" lunch. Afterwards, in an effervescent mood, we mounted skyward in our lumbering old bomber and played " hide and seek " in the clouds with a couple of scout machines from a neighbouring squadron.

Two nights before the Hun offensive opened I was detailed for a railway reconnaissance to Valenciennes with Lieutenant C——, my own pilot being temporarily indisposed. We started, but thick weather developed over the lines and we had to return. On the following night, however, we succeeded in getting there, ascertaining the train movements and silencing an "onion" battery

Before the Offensive

which was "hating" us with uncomfortable and unusual accuracy.

After we had landed we were told we should not be required again, and that we could turn in for the night; instead we walked across the fields towards the Canadian Hospital at A——, where I had been a patient during my "gravel-crunching" days, and which I wanted to see again.

It was a clear, still night, and the only sounds which met our ears were the sinister hoots of owls in the wood of Habarque and the distant rumbling of the guns. A big ammunition convoy was moving along the main Arras road, and we watched the men as they moved about in the shifting lights of their torches and lanterns. The sky was powdered with diamond-pointed stars. But imperceptibly the outlines became vaguer, began to dissolve, faded away. A night-mist drifted in from the sea over the Flanders lowlands. The moon-haze over the lines seemed tinged with blood. We turned back across the fields towards the sheen of our camp-fires over the ridge.

CHAPTER XXI

A STRENUOUS NIGHT

ABOVE us rode a high, white moon; below us was the incredible desolation of the Somme—miles on miles of craters and shell-holes, blown-in trenches, and abandoned gun-pits—a vast, abominable expanse of pain and death. We had just crossed the valley of the Ancre. The Somme lay ahead, a thin, silvery snake of a river, curving away into the night. Beneath us, in these tragic fields, lay villages and towns for ever sacred to the memory and valour of British troops—Beaumont-Hamel, Pozières, Miraumont, Bapaume.

Across the low hills and over the valleys the roads ran in long, straight ribbons, converging on Bapaume and Péronne and Albert. Beyond Albert lay Amiens and the gate to Paris. That was the direction of the German thrust, and all their roads of communication were packed with moving columns of supplies and troops.

Early that morning we had received the news

A Strenuous Night

that the German hordes were advancing; that our fellows, fighting gloriously, were slowly yielding ground; and that the issue of the battle lay to a very large extent in our hands.

All that day our scouts and bombers and fighting machines had been out, flying low, firing into the German masses as they advanced, bombing their reserves, disorganising their communications.

Now it was our turn. The day-flyers were resting. We were carrying on their work.

The roads, white in the moonshine, were packed with black silhouettes—lorries, Staff cars, guns being hurried forward, and moving companies of men.

From a height of two thousand feet, as we flew southward to the Somme, we could see three large and a number of smaller fires burning—dumps, farmhouses, stores of food and forage, munitions, engineers' material, the impedimenta of war—for the most part stuff which our fellows could not take back with them in their retreat, and which they had blown up in order to prevent its falling into the enemy's hands.

Bapaume was on fire. There was also a vast

horseshoe of flame near the Miraumont railway, while farther south and east Péronne cast skywards a shower of sparks and smoke, which, like a great blast furnace, every now and then reddened and glowed and sent up long, curling flames, licking the sky greedily.

We sighted our first target in the glare of an adjacent fire—a column of troops on the road, sandwiched in between two long convoys. We dived and flew over that long, straight road at a height of a hundred feet or less. There were gun-limbers and motor-lorries which could not leave the road, and hundreds of pygmy black figures scurrying away on each side into the shell-torn wilderness through which the road ran. Our bombs—small, savage fellows designed for infantry strafing—burst in a line along the road, and only two or three of them fell wide. We were so near the ground that we heard their detonations as one hears a salvo of guns when standing near a field battery in the line. Doubtless the horses were rearing and plunging; some of the men were probably shouting orders; others, stricken with panic, were tramping and pushing their comrades to one side and flinging themselves into shell-

A Strenuous Night

craters or trenches. Upon many of them Death had laid his violent, implacable hand.

That there was confusion and panic was obvious. There was practically no retaliation from the ground. We turned back along the road, zigzagging across it from one end of the convoy to the other, spraying the dismayed, tumultuous mass with tracer bullets from our Lewis gun.

The impression left on my mind is that of a grotesque dream—the glare of the burning village, the pygmy troops with their pygmy wagons, the sense of immense speed which one always has when flying near the ground, the bursts of flame from my gun; above it all the strong shine of the moon revealing a narrow ribbon of road stretching away and ahead through a desolate waste of shell-holes as far as the eye could reach.

Then we flew home to listen to great tales from our other flyers. One had started a big fire in a group of rest billets; another had chanced upon a German lorry-park, bombed it vigorously, and, so far as he could see, inflicted great damage; two of our pilots had blown up big guns by the roadside; several had attacked troop-trains steaming up to railheads.

Rovers of the Night Sky

We left the aerodrome on our second "show" just before eleven o'clock. Everybody was keen on getting in as many trips as possible that night. The big battle was in full swing, and we felt that it was "up to us" to do all we could for our comrades in the trenches.

Most of us had been in the infantry before joining the Flying Corps, and there is no job of work which the average flying officer likes better than troop-strafing on the roads behind the German lines. That is because he knows that this particular work is of the most direct assistance to the infantry. Reconnaissances or the bombing of factories, railways, and aerodromes miles behind the line are useful jobs, and of vital importance; yet there is not the same joy in them, because their results are not so immediately apparent to our friends in the front line. On the other hand, the work done in the battle zone from low altitudes demoralises the enemy infantry, and proportionately encourages our own.

In the Somme area, during that strenuous period, we obtained evidence from prisoners of enormous material and moral damage inflicted on the enemy by low-flying bombing machines, par-

A Strenuous Night

ticularly by night-flyers, who, under cover of darkness, are naturally able to get farther back than the day people do, and can thus attack and disorganise the German reserves and transport on the roads.

Therefore, from dusk that night until dawn the following morning, we carried on with our work of bombing and machine-gunning troops in the German forward and reserve positions; and there is no doubt that the work done by both night and day squadrons during the early days of the great Hun offensive materially hindered the enemy's plans, delayed his counter-attacks, and helped our own and the French armies on the ground eventually to stem the tide of the advance and to stabilise the position.

My pilot and I, in all our flying experience together, had never had so much excitement crowded into such a limited space of time. We did five trips of about an hour's duration each that night, and upon each occasion we chanced on targets such as we had never had before. During these operations every machine in the squadron held a roving commission.

Within a certain well-defined area we could fly

where we liked, our orders consisting only in getting down low and attacking any troops, guns transport, or trains we might see.

On our fourth trip we nearly bumped into a Boche observation balloon floating serenely in the moonlight. We were, roughly, three thousand yards behind their advanced positions—there was no definite line at that stage of the battle—and as it was only an hour or so before daybreak, we concluded that the Huns intended to steal a march on our ground folk and get their K.B.s going in time to observe our dawn movements—perhaps even in the hope of catching the last of our ration and ammunition convoys on their way back from the forward positions. There is always a good deal of movement behind the lines just after nightfall and at dawn.

My pilot saw the balloon before I did. I happened at that moment to be comparing a bend in the road, over which we were flying, with the same bend as shown on my map, and when he gave me the " look-out " signal we were within fifty yards of the phenomenon. It was slightly above our level and so bloated did it look that my first idea was we were about to fly into a cloud. Then a slight alteration

A Strenuous Night

in perspective, as we swung clear, enabled me to see the balancing-fins and the observation basket. In two seconds I had trained my gun and fired a burst. I believe that the observer was either killed or seriously wounded, though the shadow cast by the swaying gasbag above hindered my view. Both of us, however, had a fleeting impression of a figure —vague, goggled, and muffled up in heavy flying kit—falling backwards into the car.

Then we climbed above the balloon, and I dropped a couple of bombs, which missed the outer edge of its envelope and exploded near the hauling-in winch on the ground. We circled round, firing continuously. The balloon began rapidly to lose height. Evidently the people on the ground were attempting to haul it in. Eagerly we waited for the explosion, but it never came; instead, the envelope rapidly deflated, collapsed, and fell to the ground. Then they got a machine-gun near the winch into action against us, but we sprinkled the remainder of our bombs round it, and the firing died away.

We returned to the aerodrome, reloaded, and, in a heavy ground-mist which came up just before dawn, set off on our fifth " show."

At six o'clock that morning, when all the machines were back, the C.O. came into the mess.

"Well, you may 'wash-out' now!" he said. "You've put up a splendid show, you fellows, and this is what I call 'the end of a perfect night.'"

CHAPTER XXII

TWO TRAGEDIES

DURING the later nights of the Amiens offensive we flew for the most part in mist and clouds. We often stood on the aerodrome late in the afternoon and watched the scout-patrols come in, flying low over the trees and telegraph poles which border the long, straight, white road which leads up to Arras and the line. Sometimes the mist would get so thick that they had to fire up coloured rockets and Verey lights to guide their machines back to the aerodrome.

Then our turn would come. Flying in clouds and mist is no joke by day; at night the difficulties are intensified a thousandfold. The pilot watches his "pittot" tube—or speed indicator—grimly. Everything depends on this and his compass. He must keep an "even keel"; if he banks too much or uses too much rudder, and then tries to make "corrections," he discovers in a very short space of time that he scarcely knows whether he is flying right side up or upside-down—no enviable state of things that!

He will suddenly find his speed indicator registering 100-110-120, at which moment he is bound to feel "windy" to a certain extent, for these figures mean that he is diving rapidly earthwards; and he has, of course, no adequate idea how near the earth may be. The best thing to do in these circumstances is to centralise all your controls, take your hands off the "stick," keep the rudder dead straight, and let the machine get herself out. In nine cases out of ten any stable machine—and night-flying machines are very stable—will do this and fly level again of its own accord.

That is what flying in dangerous weather is like. It is risky, and it taxes your powers and capabilities to the utmost. But it is worth doing. The German flying men rarely do it; they believe in "safe" flying. And that is why our Chief in France hit the right nail on the head when he wired home that the flying boys had their "tails well up."

In this sort of weather an airman does not worry so much about ordinary flying risks as about getting lost and being compelled to make a

Two Tragedies

forced landing in unknown country. Night-flying machines are generally rigged to climb slightly with hands off the "stick," and to fly level with the throttle half closed. I remember on one occasion I flew in the day-time with a pilot who was particularly proud of the perfect rigging of his machine, and in order to demonstrate its capabilities he centralised all his controls, then stood on his seat and let the machine fly itself. In this way, without touching either "'stick," rudder, or throttle, we flew from St. Valery, at the mouth of the Somme, up to Abbeville, a distance of between ten and fifteen miles. During the whole of this flight we never deviated from the long, straight canal which leads from Abbeville to the coast.

In the day-time, on a machine as stable as that, a forced landing is merely a matter of judgment and skill, but at night-time it is entirely a question of luck. The skill of the pilot counts only in a very minor degree. You can generally succeed in crashing a machine without hurting yourself or your observer very much, provided you can keep the tail down. If the under-carriage strikes an obstacle on the ground it usually parts company with the rest of the machine, and the latter sits down quite comfortably on its wings. But if the nacelle—that is the front portion of the machine—hits anything, the sudden resistance to flight is transmitted right through the machine, almost invariably the nose remains where it struck, and as the other parts of the machine try violently to continue their flight the tail rises, swings over and crashes down on the reverse side. Before the occupants know what has happened the machine is on her back. During this process the engine often leaves its bearings, bumps through the slight partition which divides it from the pilot's seat, and, by reason of its own weight and the machine's momentum, buries itself several inches into the ground. If the pilot and the observer have not previously been thrown clear in the crash they are pinned or buried under the engine, and often either killed or very seriously injured. Occasionally also at the moment of impact the connections in the petrol system are broken, or one of the tanks bursts, spilling and spraying the liquid over the heated engine. There is a sudden flash, and in three or four seconds the machine is a blazing furnace.

One fine spring afternoon I saw an incident

Two Tragedies

of this all too frequent type. One of our pilots, who had had several bad crashes, had expressed a desire to transfer from "pusher" to "tractor" machines. An ancient B.E.—a type which rendered yeoman service in its day, but which is now obsolete—was wheeled out on to the aerodrome for him. Poor old "Binks," in helmet and goggles, but with no flying coat, strolled over to the machine and got in. His Flight Commander explained the chief cardinal differences between this type and the type he had been accustomed to fly before. We heard him say, "Take her off firmly, old man; don't forget she lifts her own tail up; and when you're landing come in at '65, put her tail down and *keep it down*."

"Binks" ran his engine up, taxied down the aerodrome, turned into wind, opened his throttle, and came with terrific speed towards the hangars. He had apparently forgotten that his tail was off the ground, for he put his joy-stick slightly forward, her nose went down, and the machine nearly turned over. He got her out of that trouble, however, and just cleared the sheds by inches. At three hundred feet he turned down the wind, and from that moment seemed to lose all control.

We believe that he fainted, because he was a good pilot and had six months' active service flying to his credit. The machine staggered back across the aerodrome, " swinging " badly. We all felt that she was an aimless and directionless piece of mechanism. The mind which should have controlled and guided her had been stricken down. Her right wing was suddenly jerked up by some aerial billow. For a moment she seemed to hang there, poised in the sunlight. She side-slipped a little way, then got her nose down and fell vertically. The sound of the crash and the sudden up-blazing of petrol were coincident. When we got there a minute later there was nothing but a smoking heap of debris.

These are two of the chief dreads of the airman—to crash and take fire before he can extricate himself from his machine; or to find himself on fire in the air, and before he can hope to save himself to have to bring a burning mass of wood and metal down to the ground and land it.

In my infantry days I remember that one evening, when I had just taken over a line of trench, I heard a distant pop-pop like the drawing of far champagne corks in the sky.

Two Tragedies

Outlined against the stormy evening sunlight were four aeroplanes rolling and diving and side-stalling round each other. One, I could see, was a British artillery observation machine, its wireless aerial trailing behind it; the others were fast German scouts.

I stood in the trench, leaning against the parados, and watched this drama of the sky fulfil itself in tragedy. It was all over within the space of a couple of minutes or so. The Briton had no chance. Had he perhaps dived down two or three thousand feet he might possibly have got out of the fight and been able to take cover behind our "archie" barrage. But he stayed gallantly and fought.

The sky was filled with the sharp, continuous resonance of machine-gun bullets. From each of the aeroplanes came vicious little spurts of smoke.

Quite suddenly the spurts from the British plane ceased, and it seemed as if a flash of lightning passed from one end of the machine to the other. For two or three seconds a tiny red spark glowed in front of the Britisher's engine, then the whole machine from propeller to tail-planes burst into flames. It flew on steadily for a hundred yards or so—a burning coffin, for nothing could possibly have lived in that violence of flame—and then dived vertically to earth.

For a minute or two the fallen aeroplane, lying just behind our lines, cast skywards its offering of flame and sparks. I ordered a corporal and two men to leave the trenches and follow me to this place of the dead hopes of two young heroes.

When we arrived there we found that the machine had burned itself out. Nothing remained except a few charred spars and wires and scraps of twisted metal. The observer, a good-looking boy, lay on his back some yards from the machine. He had evidently been flung clear in the final impact. He was comparatively untouched by flame and had been killed by the crash. The corpse of the pilot—black and unrecognisable—lay amid the cinders of his machine.

Night fell soon after that. Next morning, in the first grey of the dawn, a German aeroplane dived down on the charred wreckage. I wondered if he had been the victor in that fight, that terrible gallant struggle against odds which I had witnessed just a few hours before. If so, he had his triumph in that pitiable heap of twisted steel.

CHAPTER XXIII

AERIAL COMBATS IN THE MOONLIGHT

WILL there ever be serious fighting in the air at night-time?

I have often been asked to give my opinion as to the possibilities of night fighting in the near future, and have always replied that aerial combats of the type that we are accustomed to in the daytime are impossible by night. On dark or semi-dark nights you cannot see a machine until you are close to it. During over six months' night-flying in France I have never seen a machine on a dark night long enough to enable me to aim my gun and fire. On several occasions a machine has passed close to us, been vaguely visible for a fraction of a second, and then been lost to view completely.

One very dark night, five thousand feet over Ypres, a giant Gotha whizzed underneath us. For one brief moment I glimpsed its twin engines and long fuselage in the tiny cone of light sent down by our tail-lamp. I signalled my pilot round immediately, and we turned sharply on a vertical bank; but to look for a machine, even a big Gotha, on a dark night is as hopeless as to search for a drop of fresh water in the ocean. You might come across it by chance, but there can be no question of skill or the use of method in finding it. For this reason, fighting in the air on dark nights by means of fast-moving aeroplanes may be considered impossible.

There remains the question of moonlight nights. Here the answer cannot be given so definitely. Attempts have been made by all the belligerent Powers to bring about aerial combats in the moonlight, and there is little doubt but that in the course of time a good night-fighting machine will be evolved. The present types of heavy bombing machines are obviously unsuited for offensive fighting, although some of them could render a good account of themselves from a defensive point of view.

England can claim the first notable success so far as aerial night-fighting is concerned. It is no secret, either to our own or the German authorities, that the last great moonlight raid on London

Aerial Combats in the Moonlight

failed partly because of the accuracy and violence of our barrage, and partly because our home-defence airmen, flying fast and handy scouts and fighters, were able to bring down a number of the enemy bombers.

One of our most famous scout pilots, in order to test a theory which he had formed, went up one moonlight night and flew up and down the lines between Arras and Albert looking for machines. He saw over a dozen of our own night-bombers, but no enemy machines; in some cases he was able to get right up to a machine without being observed. A few days later he flew over to our squadron and was able to tell us the identification numbers of two or three of our machines which had crossed that sector on the night of his experiment. He had seen these numbers shining clearly in the moonlight.

During the same moonlight period our own and another night-flying squadron were attacked in the air. But the attacks were not pressed home with any determination, and we lost no machines. All this goes to show that serious night-fighting between machines equally, or nearly equally, matched can undoubtedly take place, but only under very favourable conditions of weather and visibility, and with pilots selected for exceptionally keen sight, steady nerves and accurate judgment of distances.

When anywhere near another machine at night-time you have to estimate your distance even more accurately than in daylight. An error of a fraction of an inch may spell all the difference between life and death, victory or defeat.

I remember one clear moonlight night shortly after the Cambrai stunt, when the air seemed to be—as a Canadian pilot phrased it—"lousy with German machines."

Our day-flyers had spotted a new German aerodrome which, by its area and the size of its hangars, was obviously intended for use by large night-bombing machines. The job of strafing the place was allotted to our squadron.

It was a splendid opportunity, conditions were favourable, our fellows were as keen as mustard, and we made a good night's job of it. We flew in two relays—eighteen machines before dinner and eighteen after. A week or so later, through an Intelligence source, we learned that so effective had our bombing been that two out of three

Aerial Combats in the Moonlight

Gotha flights had been forced to abandon the aerodrome, and that the damage to machines, hangars, and personnel had been very heavy. Most of the hangars had disappeared, while the aerodrome itself was thickly besprinkled with bomb-holes.

We were second off the ground that night. It was an evening of wonderful moonshine, and we were able to hang on to the tail of the first machine until we were well over the lines. Then we lost sight of it. On arrival at the target we saw our first machine at about three hundred feet above the aerodrome. The observer was firing his gun into the hangars, and being " hated " vigorously by a Boche machine-gun cleverly emplaced near some cross-roads.

The Germans had their night-landing flares out. We could see several of their machines on the ground, and they were sending up signal lights, evidently warning their own machines which were still up to keep away until our raid was over.

I stood on my locker and looked back over our tail. The air seemed full of machines, some of which were obviously German night-bombers returning from a raid over our territory. Several more of our own fellows had by now arrived on the scene. Bombs were dropping on and near the hangars; observers were firing their guns from all angles into the doomed buildings; I saw one of our machines flying low over a big German bus which, with a view to escaping from the rain of bombs and bullets, was attempting to "take off" the aerodrome.

There was a tiny red flash, a distant report almost like the drawing of a champagne cork, and then a second or two later a sudden up-blazing of petrol. For some little time that Boche machine burned furiously, lighting up hangars, workshops and hutments, and materially helping us in our work of destruction.

On our second visit later that same night the aerodrome was in darkness. There were no flares and no signalling lamps. The only sign of activity was a violent increase of "hate," the Germans having evidently brought up some mobile anti-aircraft batteries.

On the following night we again passed over this Gotha lair on our way to a more distant target in the north of Belgium. I was carrying "Little Bertha." At that time ours was the only machine

Aerial Combats in the Moonlight

in any night-flying squadron upon which this gun was mounted. Naturally, we were not a little proud of it, and as we flew over the Gothadrome I fired off a couple of shells by way of greeting. There was no reply. We learned subsequently that the aerodrome had been temporarily evacuated.

One of the most curious flying coincidences I know of occurred during the opening of the German offensive last March. In those days the enemy was very persistently bombing our back areas, and at the same time attempting raids on London and Paris. The observer in one of our machines, when well over the lines, suddenly saw a twin-engined machine flying about two hundred feet beneath him, its vast expanse of wing and long, narrow fuselage gleaming in the moonlight. Realising that this was a Gotha, and that by the route it was taking it was probably on the homeward journey from England, he decided to follow it back to its aerodrome and attempt to destroy it when landing. Meanwhile, another of our pilots farther south had encountered a Gotha which in his opinion was homeward-bound from Paris.

The London Gotha landed at an aerodrome a

mile or so to the north of X; the Paris Gotha landed at an aerodrome a little to the east of the same village. And both Gothas were destroyed, within a few miles of each other, by bombs dropped from the air while they were taxi-ing up to their hangars.

Comparing notes afterwards, it transpired that the two pairs of pilots and observers had each seen their victims at, roughly, the same distance beneath them; had been able to follow closely without the presence of their own machines being noticed; they had seen the same recognition signals flashed from the Hun aerodromes, and had followed their quarry slowly down until it was on the ground before releasing their bomb.

That was a unique bag for one night. As an airman, however, I cannot help but imagine myself in the position of the occupants of those unlucky German machines. I can see Eitel, the pilot, looking at his watch.

"Been a cold trip to-night, eh, Fritz?" he shouts to his observer. "And what a barrage over London! Mein Gott! But now we're down, my boy; we're *home!*"

They had been from four to five hours in the

Aerial Combats in the Moonlight

air; had crossed the lines twice, and been "hated" savagely each time; had braved the sea, the coast patrols, and the guns of London. Now they were down, their landing wheels had touched the ground, they remembered that in the mess there were bottles of real old beer from Munich, and —a British bomb completed the story!

CHAPTER XXIV

THE HUNS BOMB US

EARLY in April my pilot—after nine continuous months of night-flying—was transferred to the Home Establishment as an instructor. I went down to Boulogne with him in the squadron car, and we had a jolly dinner together. About midnight I started back for the aerodrome, a four hours' journey along the Etaples-Montreuil-Hesdin road, and thence through St. Pol nearly up to Arras. The Germans were shelling St. Pol with heavy stuff as we passed through it shortly before three o'clock that morning. We opened up and raced away from the place on to the Arras road, which was crowded with troops going up to the line. Just before dawn we arrived back at the aerodrome. The C.O. and Recording Officer had just turned in, having waited up all night hoping the weather would clear sufficiently to justify sending off a raid on a short target.

On the following evening I was detailed for

The Huns Bomb Us

duty as Flares Officer. It was a clear, brisk night, with a diamond-powdered sky and a crescent moon. Standing in the centre of the aerodrome, I could see the gun flashes in a wide arc round the horizon. We were then near the apex of a big triangular salient, and it often seemed as if the enemy was behind as well as in front of us. Hun machines were exceptionally active that night. They came over soon after nightfall, and evidently intended to carry on all night. Bombs were dropped on neighbouring fields and villages, and, from telephone messages received from other parts of the country, it soon became apparent that the principal German objectives that night were our British night-flying aerodromes.

Our turn came a few minutes after midnight. I had noticed a strange machine circling round the aerodrome at a height of about four thousand feet. It passed across the face of the moon, a sinister silhouette, and I knew it then for what it was—a big German night-bomber. I immediately had all the lights on the aerodrome put out, and issued instructions to the flare party not to permit any machine to land. Unfortunately, however, one of our own machines came over the Arras road, flying low, and frantically flashing down a priority distress signal. I watched the Hun turn into wind, the drone of his twin-motors now louder and more menacing. Our " bus " was gliding in over the trees at the far end of the aerodrome; still I dared not switch on the landing flares for fear of giving the exact position of the aerodrome away to the Hun bombers. All I felt I could safely do was to shine a small signalling lamp on to the part of the aerodrome where our man should touch ground. He appeared suddenly to have realised that the Huns were about and to be acting accordingly, for he put out all his navigation lights and attempted a landing in the dark, but overshot and had to go round again. At the second attempt, however, he pulled off a "pukka" landing. But the Hun had seen him, and a few seconds later dropped a big bomb near the hangars of a day-flying scout squadron which shared the aerodrome with us. A sentry on guard was badly wounded and died on the way to hospital. The windows of several huts were shattered by the concussion, but the chief damage was represented by a vast bomb-crater in front of the hangars.

Several smaller bombs peppered the road which

The Huns Bomb Us

bordered the aerodrome, and then another huge fellow came singing down. We flung ourselves flat on the ground. It is no good standing up and shaking your fist at a two-hundred-and-fifty-pound bomb travelling towards you at the rate of a thousand miles an hour. If you lie down, except for a direct hit, you are tolerably safe from flying fragments of bomb-casing; if you don't lie down you run the risk of getting a chunk of shrapnel through your head.

The bomb burst in our transport lines and "wrote off" a three-ton lorry.

Realising that the Hun had now located and was attacking our aerodrome in earnest, we made a dash for the sandbagged machine-gun positions. Our anti-aircraft defences had opened up and the sky was filled with bursting shells. The Hun, who seemed to be quite a daring fellow, came lower, and once or twice we caught a glimpse of him at between a thousand and fifteen hundred feet. We got off thousands of rounds of tracer bullets at him, and in the region where, by the sound of his engines, we estimated him to be; but he must have had a very useful mascot on board, for he just sailed on and continued merrily to drop his bombs. He churned up the road in several places; he destroyed an unoffending farmhouse three quarters of a mile from the aerodrome; he annihilated numbers of turnips; and he "put the wind up" several horses which had gone to sleep in the fields. We suffered no casualties, the scout squadron had only one; the damage to the aerodrome consisted of bomb-holes which were filled up in less than a day.

While the Hun was bombing us two of our machines attempted to land in the dark. One of them "arrived" in a ditch and turned over, throwing both pilot and observer clear; the other sat down heavily and wiped off its under-carriage.

At dawn the Hun sheered off, and we went to bed.

CHAPTER XXV

THE STORY OF THE PRISONERS' CAGE

THE Huns attempted further raids on several successive evenings, but never again got within a mile of the aerodrome. One of their machines crashed badly near St. Pol, all its occupants being killed. I was flying that night with my new pilot, one of the pluckiest and cheeriest fellows in the squadron. We were in a reckless mood, and got down to between three and four hundred feet.

Bapaume and many of the villages round it were on fire; there was also a big blaze in the railway cutting near Miraumont. We dropped our bombs on old British billets at Vaulx, then occupied by the advancing Huns, then flew round the Bapaume area, machine-gunning the roads. On the way home I took the "stick," and for nearly ten minutes controlled the machine from the front seat.

We did three "shows" that night, had tea and eggs in the mess on our return from the last trip, and turned in just as the day-flyers were starting on their dawn patrols. We got up in time for lunch, however, and, being in the humour for it, spent the whole of the afternoon flying about the country, landing at two or three aerodromes, stunting over the grounds of the big Canadian Hospital at A——, and concluding the performance by flying up to Vimy and watching the shell-bursts on the ridge. On our return my pilot landed the machine, then we changed seats, and I taxied it into the hangars. For a first attempt at taxi-ing—more difficult than most people imagine—the experts told me that it was not bad.

That same evening I flew with the C.O. Our objective was the town of Bray-sur-Somme, which the Germans had captured a day or two earlier. The Somme roads were crowded with troops and transport, and we wished we could have carried more ammunition. There was no "hate"; evidently the Huns had not yet had time to organise their anti-aircraft defences in these recently captured areas. The C.O. was in great form.

"It's money for nothing," he declared as we walked up to the mess after the "show." "Not a single 'archie'; not even machine-guns."

The Story of the Prisoners' Cage

He must have enjoyed himself, because he stood me a couple of drinks and insisted on calculating the number of Germans we had probably put out of action as a result of our night's work.

On the following evening, while flying with our new Flight-Commander, I started a really big fire. It was probably a petrol dump, and the reflection of its glare could be seen many miles away on our side of the lines. On landing from this "show" the joyful news was communicated to me that my leave had come through, and that on the morrow I should start for Blighty.

Just before I left the aerodrome *en route* for England I heard a " priceless " story of one of the results of our recent bombing. The account came through the usual Intelligence channels, and may be relied upon. It concerned the escape of several British soldiers from a German cage for prisoners near Irles. One of our night-bombers was heard in the distance, throbbing its way across the night sky. From all accounts, it was flying very low, and as it approached the Huns on guard at the cage began to show signs of panic. They had evidently made the acquaintance of British night-flyers before. Presently bombs fell and exploded a quarter of a mile down the road. The Hun guards threw themselves prone on the ground in an agony of apprehension. In their extreme terror they completely forgot the prisoners they were supposed to be guarding.

Finally a big bomb burst in the roadway immediately outside the cage.

In the graphic words of the escaped Tommy who related the story, " That put the lid on it, sir. Every Fritzy within a mile of that bomb ran to cover, and we just walked out of the cage and strolled down the road. Some of the boys were caught again, but a good many of us were lucky enough to get through the lines and so back to our units."

This story both amused and delighted us; and we were glad to find out later from the Wing records that it must have been one of our own squadron machines which had effected this deliverance of some of our infantry comrades from durance vile. There was naturally a good deal of friendly rivalry as to whose was the actual machine which had dropped the freedom-dealing bombs. But this we were never able satisfactorily to decide.

CHAPTER XXVI

HOW ENGLAND GOES TO WAR

THE return-leave train—that war-time institution of our national life—is worth a word or two. Every family in the land has seen it, either in reality or in vision, steaming away from Victoria into the Unknown Country.

There is a Staff train in the afternoon, but one does not associate poignancy with red tabs. You will see the real leave-takings if you go to Victoria in the raw of the morning. Subalterns, sergeants, sappers, company commanders, and cooks travel by this early special to France.

The afternoon train is filled with concentrated B's—Brigadiers, Brass-hats, Brigade-Majors; and with them a sprinkling of nurses, V.A.D.s, politicians proceeding Paris-wards, " Waacs," journalists travelling to Headquarters for a " conducted " tour of the front, financiers, pacifists, spies, and larger and smaller fry of all varieties.

This being the account of an ordinary R.A.F.

bird, we are not concerned with the Staff train. We have seen it. Some day we hope to ride in it. Let us, therefore, return to the Tommies' special, to our corporals and cooks, to the men who will live with us the life of trench or billet.

An hour and a half before its time of departure some of them begin to arrive—drafts from Ireland and the North, Australians, Canadians, men from the counties and from London, little groups of sleep-heavy soldiers, slung around with the amazing impedimenta of war—packs, gas-masks, shrapnel-helmets, water-bottles, bandoliers, wallets—all of which go to the make-up of the British soldier's field equipment.

We stand about on the platform, smoking, chatting, furtively eyeing those who are to be our travelling companions, avoiding the eyes of mother and sweetheart, putting up a fine pretence of cheerfulness. The crowd begins to thicken. The atmosphere grows heavy with cheap smoke. Military police prowl up and down. Officers begin to report to the R.T.O., and the long train gradually fills.

You know these awkward partings—tremulous, deep thoughts unsaid, hopes unexpressed, brave attempts at nonchalance; over it all the sense of Kismet. Your subaltern who has been "out" before affects an air of boredom, strolls along the platform emitting whiffs of "gold flake," regards with derision the obviously new hand.

The breakfast-saloons exhale appetising odours of coffee and bacon. Several hardened subs have already taken their places at the tables and are ordering their meals with magnificent unconcern. Outside on the platform the last good-byes are spoken; but not with words. Blighty seems very dear during these final tender-bitter moments. Youth is calling to love and life. But there is a grim job to do. And all the world seems grey.

Finally, the long train glides quietly away from the platform. There is a weird suggestion of finality about as it rolls over Grosvenor Bridge and disappears round the bend by Battersea.

We grow cheerful after breakfast. Youth is youth after all; and there is adventure ahead.

"What part of the line are you going to?" says one old stager to another.

"Oh, the same merry old spot—the salient," replies the other.

"What a mess of a place! I had six months at Wipers!"

The conversation, couched for the main part in lurid expletives, becomes reminiscent. The two discover mutual friends in the train, and for the last hour of the run they play bridge.

Thus does England go to war.

In the train I met an Old Bill of a fellow, a Canadian captain, late a rancher in Western Canada. Before this encounter I had steadfastly refused to believe in the existence of men of the Old Bill type. Now I know that there are a few of them knocking about here and there. Only about one man in ten thousand, however, possesses the unique turn of mind of Bairnsfather's creation; and when you find him he is "priceless."

This Canadian captain, whom, by a strange turn in the wheel of fortune, I subsequently met in the trenches, was one such.

Three of us were sitting at a table in the breakfast-saloon. The train was rolling through Kent. In half an hour we should be on the boat. I was silent; lost in long thoughts of home, friends, that last night in the Big Village, the bravery shining through a dear woman's eyes, the tender passion of her lips.

On the opposite side of the table, by the side of my Canadian, sat a pale, inquisitive youth, obviously a Londoner, who was frankly apprehensive as to what was going to happen to him on the other side of the Channel. The Canadian was equally frank. But his was the frankness of experience, not ignorance. He was as blasé as the traditional Old Bill. He jerked and snapped out his remarks in such a manner that a less persistent inquirer than my little Cockney would have given the game up in disgust.

"What do we do on landing in Boulogne?" the pale youth demanded.

"Follow the other two thousand of us, sonny. Some guys report to the M.L.O. Not me! The Hôtel du Louvre for this child. Every time!"

"What about one's kit?"

"Kit!" ejaculates the Canadian. "Don't tell me you're bringing *kit* to France. I thought you were a G-dd-d soldier."

The Londoner's spirits were damped for a few moments, during which he eyed the Canadian furtively. He decided eventually that his leg was being pulled rather elaborately, and for the space of a full minute he relapsed into silence. Presently, however, the silence, or the Canadian's rank cigar, or both, became too much for him.

"If we have to stay the night in Boulogne, are there officers' quarters?" he burst out at last.

"Lord!" said the Canadian grimly, "you must be the kind of guy who'll expect flowers on his grave."

Then he laughed. But when the train pulled up alongside the quay in Folkestone harbour, and emptied its freight of fighting men into the long grey ship which was waiting there, he said not unkindly :

"Come down to the bar, kid, and have a drink. Guess I can tell you all you'll want to know."

What a mysterious old lady the Sea is! She always reminds me of a certain old dame whom I once knew and admired very much. She could be as inscrutable as the Sphinx and as talkative as a young hen with her first brood of chicks. She possessed the strange inflexibility of nature, yet seemed often more impressionable than molten silver. She could be as cruel as sin and as wonderfully kind as a virgin in her first rapture of love. Sometimes she appeared young and transcendently beautiful, but anon she would reveal her age-old and weary heart. She was the most amazing enigma of a woman I have ever known; as deeply and incomprehensibly mysterious as the Sea.

On this grey morning the breeze stretching out from France brought with it a strange foretaste of new things, heroic visions, the " cup of Fortune and Romance always filled and brimming over, waiting only for heroes and the sons of heroes to quaff it, and drinking deeply to call for more."

We were convoyed by long vicious-looking destroyers steaming on either flank, and belching vast, protective clouds of smoke. Before we left the harbour every officer and man on board had been ordered to put on a life-belt, for only a few days before a submarine had attacked a troopship on the cross-Channel route.

Half-way across the Channel two aeroplanes, flying low, passed us and disappeared into the mist which hung over the French coast. The green, dusty haze touched the sea with a vague menace. France, looming now but a mile or two away, gave one a sinister impression, much as a house does in which a violent crime has been committed, or as the sombre portals of a prison when they close for the last time upon some desperate wretch condemned to die.

There was not much time to spare at Boulogne. Men were badly wanted in the line. The Germans were still advancing on Paris. There were rumours of " stunts " in preparation. The drafts therefore marched away up the hill to the rest-camp, while officers were ordered to report that night to the Railway Transport Officer at the *Gare Central.* Those who had been out before were to join the trains for the various Divisional railheads; newcomers were to go up by the six o'clock troop-special to the infantry base; R.A.F. people were to proceed forthwith either to their squadrons or to one of the Pools.

An hour or so before our train was due to leave a hospital train from the Amiens front steamed in, and I watched the transfer of two or three hundred battered victims of war to the ambulance cars. Later I walked down to the quay. There were two hospital ships there, one of which had already been filled. The other was being rapidly loaded with its cargo of maimed and suffering men. I spoke to one of the medical staff on the ship, and was allowed to talk to a young subaltern who three days before had been in England and was now on his way home again. He had left London on Thursday morning, arrived in the trenches on Friday night, been wounded on Saturday morning, and would reach London again that night, which was Sunday.

"It's hell up there," he said to me. "Cold, muddy, devilish uncomfortable!"

He seemed to have been impressed more by the discomfort than anything else.

"Did you get your wound in a scrap, or was it a chance shot?" I asked him.

He seemed reluctant to talk about his experiences.

"Got it in the early morning," he said at length, "during stand-to! A whiz-bang brought the parapet and the side of the trench and the whole blinking lot in on us. Three of my men were buried. As for myself—well, I stopped a bit of the shell-case with my shoulder-blade."

The boy was obviously glad to be out of the cold and the misery of it, yet chagrined that he had got his "ticket" for Blighty so soon. I told him that London had not changed much during the last three days, wished him a speedy recovery, and bade him good-bye!

On my way back to the station I reflected that this boy, who had had little or no experience of men and the world, could nevertheless claim to have come to close grips with the actualities of the most momentous crisis in the world's history. He had been in the Fire, and had come through it burned yet finely tempered. The light in his eyes and the set of his face were no longer those of a boy; they were those of a man whose metal has been tested and vindicated in the hour of supreme trial.

CHAPTER XXVII

A RACE WITH DAWN

DURING my period of leave the squadron had flown still farther south to a pretty aerodrome in the Somme country. On my arrival there I found that we lived in tents in the shadow of a big wood, and that near by were farmhouses where eggs and bread, fresh vegetables, chickens, ale and champagne could be purchased. Dame Nature had been busy during my absence. Sprays of vetch now straggled over the banks on either side of the road, their small purple flowers peeping from out the deep green of the bush. Huge white-hearts blossomed on the trees in the gardens that we passed, and in places even hung over the road. A light breeze wafted abroad the aroma of scented almonds and roses. It was altogether a delectable spot, untouched by the hand of war.

On the day following my arrival back with the squadron I was ordered to salvage kit and material from an abandoned aerodrome which the German advance had brought within a few hundred yards of the line. Standing on the ridge which overlooks the Ancre, I could see the smoking ruins of Albert and all the desolation of that tragic valley. Our shells were bursting in Thiépval Wood, and the German gunners were putting down a very heavy barrage between Martinsart and Engelbelmer. I saw a high velocity shell completely demolish a cottage less than a hundred yards from where I was standing.

An elderly officer with grey hair and a grey moustache had been standing but a moment before in the doorway of the cottage smoking a cigar. I naturally decided that he had perished in the explosion, and I was greatly astounded and relieved when, a few seconds later, he emerged from the smoking debris, covered with dust and dirt but otherwise uninjured. How he escaped death he was unable to say. He was very glad of the nip of brandy from my flask which I offered him.

We succeeded in rescuing a good deal of valuable material from the derelict aerodrome, packed it on to our lorries, and drove along a road, which was being intermittently shelled, out of the battle zone into safety. On the way home we had dinner

A Race with Dawn

in a French officers' mess, and did not reach the aerodrome until well after midnight.

There followed fourteen successive nights of flying—flying from dusk to dawn with brief intervals for reloading, rearming and refreshment. The weather, until towards the end of this period, was perfect; the shows were short, eventful, and— what is always of importance to the *moral* of a squadron—were felt to be of immediate moment to the troops in the line; and all our machines did successful work without suffering a single casualty.

One of our fellows, a hankerer after statistics, borrowed the squadron records and computed the total mileage covered by all our machines during this intense period and the aggregate weight of bombs dropped. I have forgotten the figures, but I remember that they surprised us all when they were announced; and even if only ten per cent. of the bombs dropped and the rounds of ammunition fired were effective they must have inflicted vast damage, material and moral, upon the Hun.

Among a kaleidoscopic maze of memories relating to this period three or four stand out clearly above the rest as definite and notable impressions. There is the night I flew with a transferred pilot from the R.N.A.S., who seemed to have different ideas altogether on the subject of aerial navigation from those current in the squadron. It was extraordinarily difficult to keep him for any length of time flying on the correct compass-bearing. But we got there in the end, and carried out a successful raid. He subsequently explained to me that "tacking across the compass-bearing alternately from one side to the other" was his method of keeping himself tolerably accurate and of correcting "errors of drift." I did not argue the point, he being a naval and I a military man.

Then there was the night when, while diving through the beam of a searchlight which had picked us up, an "archie" shell burst ten or fifteen yards in front of us, and a large piece of the casing smashed through the nose of the machine, missing my face by inches, then sang its way upward through the wires into outer space. I smelt the acrid, pungent smoke of the shell as we dived through the region where it had burst. Later, on landing, we found that the front seat of the machine would have to be rebuilt, and that there was a long gash in the fabric of the upper wing.

On another occasion we flew through dense

A Race with Dawn

clouds with orders to bomb a concentration of enemy troops which had been reported in a village between Albert and Bapaume. At two thousand feet the ground became invisible. We flew on a compass-bearing for a given length of time, then dropped a parachute-flare in the hope that it would reveal some recognisable feature. All it did, however, was to light up the thick, lower layers of cloud and mist which were between us and the ground. We held a rapid consultation and decided to fly on for another minute or two before definitely giving up the raid. I dropped another flare in due course, and while doing so happened to look in the direction of the first flare. It was floating serenely in the clouds about two miles away and a thousand or more feet beneath our level. *And for some unknown reason the Hun gunners were strafing it*—shelling our poor little silken parachute. The sky all round it was stabbed with sharp red bursts of shrapnel. Even to-day I cannot make up my mind as to why the Huns were so interested in our flare, unless they hoped that where the flare was there the machine would be also. A little reflection, however, would have shown them what a foolish supposition this was.

We did not find our target that night. Indeed, most of the machines had been recalled by rockets. We had got off with the first batch and were too far away, but the rest had the warning from the coast that heavy clouds were blowing up from the sea and that dangerous flying weather would develop.

On the following night we again attempted to raid that same village, but several machines got tied up in the clouds, lost their way, and had to make forced landings in different parts of the country. Our machine was among the number of those that strayed.

We left the aerodrome about an hour after midnight, flew through fog and low clouds, started our compass swinging, lost direction, and ultimately had to admit that we were lost. We climbed above the clouds and at last saw the stars. The eastern rim of the horizon paled with the coming dawn. I looked at my watch. It was nearly four o'clock. We had perhaps an hour's supply of petrol left in our tanks. Suddenly, miles ahead in the direction we were flying, I saw the violence of a dawn barrage—a big arc of gun-flashes staining the magic of the dawn.

A Race with Dawn

"We're still over Hunland," I shouted to my pilot. "We'll have to cross the lines in daylight."

As the stars went out in the east we played a game of hazard with death. It must be remembered that a night-flying machine is built not for speed but to carry weight. We knew, therefore, that unless we could regain the lines before daylight we should be at the mercy of any Hun scout who might be prowling about seeking for such prey as we would afford him.

We put our nose down and ran our engine full out. My pilot kept a keen look-out forward and beneath; I stood on my locker and watched behind and above. In this way we had all the lines of approach to our machine guarded as carefully as it was possible to guard them. Fortunately, however, the ground mist hindered observation, and we crossed the lines in safety. Then, spiralling down, we found an aerodrome, landed, inquired our way from a sleepy flight-sergeant, and flew home.

I have rarely sighted the gleam of our little white tents in the shadow of the wood with so much relief as I did that misty, sunny spring morning.

CHAPTER XXVIII

FOR WHAT DID HE DIE?

AFTER that the weather broke up utterly and uncompromisingly. It rained all day and all night, the wind rose to gale force, and not an aeroplane in the whole of France dared to show its nose outside its hangar. And then occurred the inevitable reaction from the strain and tension of the preceding fortnight.

Festivities commenced early in the evening. Dinner was a jolly affair. We had had a consignment of fresh fish from Abbeville, and there were cutlets of luscious veal, new potatoes and green vegetables. The sweet was excellent, and our mess president even " put on " a savoury. The corks began to fly as the orderlies fortified and refortified our tumblers with wine from Rheims and Epernay. Afterwards—well, there were liqueurs and two cases of pre-war whisky to be consumed.

Someone started the gramophone the while

For What Did He Die?

someone else played on the piano; in the corner, through all the rising din, four stalwarts endeavoured to "carry on" with a game of bridge.

A sudden scrimmage developed, however, and the card party disappeared in the ensuing mêlée.

One merchant, who persisted in declaiming a poem called "Lasca," and who stated that he wanted "free life and fresh air," was urged gently but forcibly through the window. There was laughter and the smashing of glassware. Rushes here succeeded rushes there. The room swayed to and fro. Chairs cracked; tables collapsed under the strain, a door gave outwards, carrying with it a merry, clutching crowd of fellows who fell in one seething, shouting heap in the mud outside.

In one moment you discovered yourself inside the bar, serving drinks; the next, unseen hands snatched you, hustled you and hurled you through the window. It was a "hot-stuff rag," and it did us all good. There was a heavy bill for damages to settle the next day, but we all paid up cheerfully. Thus does Young England at war renew and refresh itself for the struggle ahead!

The weather did not clear for more than a week. The Germans drove forward, and our fellows fell

188 Rovers of the Night Sky

back in storms of wind and rain. Daily we watched the never-ending processions of homeless refugees toiling down to the sea along the old high road between Amiens and the mouth of the Somme—driftwood on the sea of war, pitiable flotsam and jetsam driven up on a barren coast by the surging German tide.

Then the news flashed through that the Australians had held up the advance at the gates of Amiens. They had counter-attacked at Villers-Bretonneux, won through, and checked the German onrush. We were holding Arras, too, against stupendous attacks. Our line was stiffening.

The sun shone once more, and the skies of France were filled with silver wings.

Flying activities on both sides increased a hundredfold. The Huns bombed our aerodromes, billets, camps, railways, towns—and we bombed theirs. Although the German in the air can at times hit hard, we invariably hit harder; and, in the opinion of those competent to judge, during the great struggle for Amiens we gave him at least ten to one.

So put *that* in your pipes and smoke it, you doubters and waverers!

For What Did He Die? 189

Flying during a big battle taxes one's powers and capabilities to the utmost. But it is worth doing.

During the later stages of the Amiens fighting our orders were simple and concise :

"Get down low and strafe troops on the road."

We had half a dozen nights of perfect moonshine before the weather broke up again, and we made full use of them. In the daytime we tested our machines by flying to the sea and stunting over Abbeville, or Gayeux, or St. Valery, or some of the French aerodromes on the coast. At night we made a practice of getting off before dusk, gaining our height, and crossing the lines as soon as it became dark.

During this period one of our new pilots, on returning from his first show, came down in the main street of a village. Fortunately, he was thrown clear and sustained only a slight shock. His observer, however, was cut about the face rather badly and broke several bones.

A night or two later the squadron suffered its only fatal casualty during a period of six months. An engine failed, and the pilot decided to attempt a forced landing. He came down in a fairly good field, misjudged the ground, failed to "flatten out," and overturned into a ditch. His observer was pitched forward violently and broke his leg at the ankle; the pilot was pinned under the engine, which settled down. His observer—as stout an Irishman as ever breathed—crawled with his fractured leg across the field in quest of help. But when he got back to the wrecked machine his pilot was dead. A party of siege gunners from a battery in a railway cutting near by after much effort lifted the engine away, and then it was seen that in any case our comrade could not have survived his injuries.

He was a good fellow, and his end touched us all. For *what* did he die?

As I write these words I am sitting in a garden by the English sea. Over there in Flanders—a score or two of miles away—the guns are pounding. I can hear them plainly. I can sense the menace of their dull reverberations. They are the guns that are saving the world. On the other side of that mighty girdle of flame and steel sprawls the erstwhile Mailed Colossus, arrogantly bestraddling Europe. Pound away, guns of France and

For What Did He Die?

England. Belch your barrages; crump your heavies and your high velocities; speed your message home. The challenge was flung down with sneers and contempt. Let *your* answer be made in *fire and steel*. It is the only language the enemy understands.

For what did he die?

You, dear lady, who wait for your man, or perhaps have given him already as part of the price which England is paying for her soul, you know, for what he died! And you English schoolboys, who will some day " follow the trail " and be proud of the heritage your fathers and brothers have won, you will know and understand when you are older!

He died for the love of England and the sweet sound of her name, and the sane, strong things she has fought for.

CHAPTER XXIX

A MISS IS AS GOOD AS A MILE

At length the time drew near when I had to leave France and come home.

When an observer has served his apprenticeship of six or seven months of war flying in France, he is usually sent to England for a pilot's course. The experiences of observers on active service give them nerve, confidence, and judgment. Many of them become accustomed to taking control of their machines on the way home from the lines; all that they now require is a certain amount of technical instruction in engines and rigging, and, of course, plenty of actual flying practice in all kinds of weather. Old observers usually develop into careful, steady, and successful pilots. They have learnt to fly in the best school of all—the school of experience, accustoming themselves gradually to the sensations of flying, learning danger at first-hand, listening to the yarns and dodges of old pilots.

A Miss is as Good as a Mile

A fellow who really wants to do so can learn more in a month with a squadron in France about machines and engines and flying and "hate-dodging" and fighting tactics than he can in six months at a school in England. He lives in an atmosphere in which spars, booms, tappet-rods, big and little ends, bracing wires, longerons, centre-section struts, gadgets of all kinds and for all functions, are spoken of as tea-cups and saucers might be spoken of in a drawing-room. He cannot help but assimilate little scraps of knowledge every day and all day which will be of use to him when he goes home to learn to fly.

At the same time he has discovered for himself the value of cunning. He is not so apt—as are so many schoolboys straight out from England—to "rush in where angels fear to tread." Many a brilliant pilot would be living to-day, and rendering service to his country, had he but exercised the virtues of control and restraint. *In flying the offensive spirit is essential*, but the successful fighter in the air, the man who takes the best pictures, who does the most accurate bombing, is the man who remains cool in the heat of action, who unites bravery with cunning, who figures things out beforehand, who can dodge and rapidly change his plans, and so confuse his enemies. The secret of aerial as of ground fighting is to have something in reserve of which your opponent has no knowledge, and to keep in your own hands the initiative of manœuvre.

The observer in France—whether he is fighting, bombing, taking photographs, or observing for the gunners—learns all this exactly as a baby imbibes the elements of human wisdom with its mother's milk. That is why I advise every would-be pilot, if it is possible, first to serve his apprenticeship as a war-flying observer.

It was during the Amiens stunt that my pilot and I had our narrowest escape from death. Our target that night was an important group of billets in the battle zone, between five and six miles behind the front line. Shortly after dinner we set off on our first raid. There was a good deal of ground-haze in the valleys and low-lying parts, but, in aerial parlance, the weather was "fifty-fifty" or "half-and-half," that is, it was fit for short raids.

The show proved uneventful: we met with just about the normal amount of "hate": got down

A Miss is as Good as a Mile

to a thousand feet, dropped our "pills," and flew back to our aerodrome.

While the mechanics were refilling and reloading our machine we repaired to the mess for a drink and a chat with the other fellows, little knowing that before we entered the anteroom again we were to be posted as "missing."

We left the aerodrome on our second raid shortly before midnight. The weather had become considerably worse, but as it was only a short show we did not worry much about it. Our minds were concentrated on getting out and home before the ground-mist should have thickened to such an extent as to obscure landmarks and to render landing a difficult and hazardous operation.

My pilot ran his engine full out up to the line, then throttled-back into a long, steady glide to enable me to guide him on to where I imagined the target to be. Then, at a given moment, we released one of our parachute flares. A few seconds later it burst from four to five hundred feet above the ground. The parachute opened up, and the flare drifted in mid-air, burning slowly and brightly, revealing in its pitiless glare the long row of huts and buildings we had come to bomb.

Almost at the same moment two other flares blazed out. Three of our machines had evidently gained the target at about the same time.

By the light of the three flares we circled in wide spirals, dropping our bombs, firing " Little Bertha," and keeping a keen look out for the other machines. Then, just as we were beginning to think once more of the grateful ease of our little tent in the wood, of coffee and sandwiches, and of bed, the machine jerked, quivered, vibrated violently; there was an explosion like the bursting of a heavy shell, and the engine clanked and jolted for a few horrible seconds, then slowly, inexorably coughed itself out.

I looked round; my pilot signalled "engine hit," and immediately swung her nose west.

To the end of my days I never shall forget that wild run for the lines. We had made use of our rapidly dropping " revs " to get a mile or so on our journey before the engine " conked " altogether, and we were forced to take up our gliding angle and look about for somewhere to land. The ground was blotted out by a thick blanket of haze, and, while I strained through it in an endeavour to see what lay beneath, my pilot " stalled " the

A Miss is as Good as a Mile

"bus" along—that is, held her up in the air at her bare flying speed.

It was impossible to make out the line with any certainty as very few Verey lights were being fired up from the trenches.

"We're down to a hundred feet. Can't keep her up any more, old boy. We've got to perch," my pilot shouted.

I fired a Verey light into the ground and waited for the crash. We banked steeply to avoid the edge of a forest, which had just loomed up through the mist, and then we were "down" amid a maze of trenches, wire, and shell-holes.

We climbed out, sat on the ground, and, being convinced that we were on the wrong side of the lines, waited for a German guard to turn up. In such moments as these you realise more fully what England and the people at home mean to you. We were discussing the surest and quickest way of getting the news through that we were safe and unwounded when a lamp was flashed at us and we heard a lusty English voice shouting distantly: "Hallo, who are you?"

Then we behaved as schoolboys do who have been granted an unexpected half-holiday.

A friendly sergeant and some men listened wonderingly to the tale of our landing. They had watched our " big machine scraping over the Boche front-line trenches with just a few feet to spare."

" If I was you, sir," said the sergeant, " I'd 'op it as quick as you can. You ain't more'n twenty yards from our front line; and we're on a bit of a ridge 'ere which Jerry shells reg'lar-like every 'arf 'our or so. What's more, sir, it'll be daylight soon, and then 'e won't 'arf pepper your machine."

We asked him if he could put a guard on the machine and take us to the nearest company-headquarters.

" I'll put a guard on, sir, certainly. But I'll 'ave to withdraw it at dawn. It won't be 'ealthy-like round these 'ere parts for an hour or two after that."

We got back to the company-headquarters just as dawn was breaking. Ten minutes later the German gunners were busy. One of their early patrols had evidently spotted the derelict bus, and signalled the " pin-points " back to their forward batteries, which had then concentrated on the target until our machine was nothing more than a heap of twisted steel and splintered fragments of wood.

About breakfast-time we got through on the 'phone to our squadron and learned that we had already been posted as "missing." The Recording Officer promised, however, to send off an urgent wire cancelling the Casualty Report.

That night we had experienced the whole gamut of flying sensations—exultation at finding our target in dark, treacherous weather; keen excitement at "getting down to it"; sudden misgivings as our engine failed us; alternating hope and despair as we struggled homeward towards our lines; racking of nerves as we waited for the impending "crash"; utter amazement to find ourselves on the ground and *alive*, even if in Hunland; finally, schoolboy reaction of delight when we discovered that we had crossed the lines after all and were among friends.

CHAPTER XXX

ADIEU!

WE did not get another machine for nearly a week after our lucky forced landing near the line; then from the aircraft depot we got one which carried an overhauled engine and was badly rigged. My pilot tested it an hour or two before our last stunt together, and, although he was not pleased with it, he decided to report it "serviceable" for a short raid.

Our operation orders that evening were to fly along the Somme valley, to note any aerodrome or train activity east of Péronne, and to bomb the great railway junction at Épéhy. We had engine trouble on the ground, and did not get off until ten minutes after all the other machines had left the aerodrome. Then, as we were not altogether satisfied with the sound of the engine, we flew for nearly twenty minutes round one of the lighthouses to give it a chance of "running itself sweet." Finally we laid our fate on the lap of St.

Adieu!

Michael, swung our nose east, and crossed the front.

It was a clear, still night. Low down on the distant horizon a sullen barrage flashed and gleamed. A crescent moon glittered against a dark background of sky. Stars and planets wandered their eternal road. It was a night of subtle sensuousness, warm, enchanting. I forgot the machine and its engine, my guns and gadgets, and dreamed of heavy perfumes in an Eastern garden, of the delicate filigree of palm-fronds against the sky, of sweet, exquisite notes sung by some unknown singer in an inner *patio*, of a girl in a soft cream gown, her fair hair waved down over her forehead, her voice low and sweet.

I was recalled from dreams to reality by the sudden violence of shrapnel bursts in the sky around us. Aveluy Wood lay beneath us, and Thiépval, and the stricken valley of the Ancre. The German batteries were firing at us from Thiépval Ridge. Away to the south a bright glare showed against the sky. A big dump had been hit, or some luckless village was casting heavenwards its offering of flame.

We made a south-easterly course to the Somme

and struck the river near Bray. The Hun night-flying aerodrome on the Bray-Suzanne road was lit up in red and green. Their flares were on, and they were firing rockets to guide their machines home. We left visiting-cards in the shape of a couple of bombs, and immediately all their lights were switched off.

Five minutes later we sighted Péronne. A few lights winked up at us from the streets of this city which had been ours for so long, and which we had but recently lost after heavy rearguard fighting. We flew into a searchlight barrage, and my pilot had to throw the machine about violently—stalling, sideslipping, diving, and "zooming"—in order to escape the cold embrace of those tentacles of light.

We crossed the Somme again and made a wide circuit round to Epéhy. The sidings and all the lines running into the big junction were full of trains. We throttled our engine down and glided to about fifteen hundred feet, then pulled our bombs. There were several good bursts on the line, but we were too high to observe the results accurately, and as our engine was rough and unreliable we did not feel justified in going down any lower.

Adieu!

On the way home our engine began to splutter and kick, the "revs" gradually dropped, and we began to think we were booked for another forced landing. We crossed the trenches at less than a thousand feet, our engine clanking and jolting like a bag of nails.

"Shall we perch?" signalled my pilot.

"No!" I replied. "Not if you think she is good for another ten miles."

We carried on, made the aerodrome, and "bumped" in. An examination of our engine revealed a broken tappet-rod.

That was my last flight as an observer. My transfer to home establishment for "instruction in aviation" had come through. I went to my tent that night half sorry to leave France, yet more than glad to bid her adieu.

London was calling me. I wanted to get back for a space to the smoke and grime of it all, the cabs and evening papers, the trams, clubs, and theatres. I wanted to feel English rain in my face; to watch the lights along the Embankment winking through swirls of mist; to see the tugs fussing seawards from London Bridge; and the Pool with the big Indiamen looming through the dusk; and Big Ben; and the Strand, and the crowds—those moving, sentimental crowds of London.

The big grey city called me, and her call was gladly answered.

www.ingramcontent.com/pod-product-compliance
Lightning Source LLC
Chambersburg PA
CBHW032111090426
42743CB00007B/314